Plant Biotechnology

The Green World

Ethnobotany

Forestry

Horticulture

Photosynthesis and Respiration

Plant Biotechnology

Plant Cells and Tissues

Plant Development

Plant Diversity

Plant Ecology

Plant Genetics

Plant Nutrition

Plant Biotechnology

William G. Hopkins

CHELSEA HOUSE
PUBLISHERS
An imprint of Infobase Publishing

Plant Biotechnology

Chelsea House
An imprint of Infobase Publishing
132 West 31st Street
New York NY 10001

Library of Congress Cataloging-in-Publication Data

Hopkins, William G.
  Plant biotechnology / William G. Hopkins.
      p. cm. — (The green world)
  Includes bibliographical references and index.
  ISBN 0-7910-8964-9 (hardcover)
  1. Plant biotechnology—Juvenile literature. I. Title. II. Green world (Philadelphia, Pa.)
  SB106.B56H67 2006
  630—dc22   2006008157

Chelsea House books are available at special discounts when purchased in bulk quantities for businesses, associations, institutions, or sales promotions. Please call our Special Sales Department in New York at (212) 967-8800 or (800) 322-8755.

You can find Chelsea House on the World Wide Web at http://www.chelseahouse.com

Text and cover design by Keith Trego and Ben Peterson

Printed in the United States of America

Bang FOF 10 9 8 7 6 5 4 3 2 1

This book is printed on acid-free paper.

All links, web addresses and Internet search terms were checked and verified to be correct at the time of publication. Because of the dynamic nature of the web, some addresses and links may have changed since publication and may no longer be valid.

Table of Contents

Introduction   vii

1 **What Is Biotechnology?**   2

2 **The Early Days of Biotechnology**   12

3 **Plants and Biotechnology**
  Before Recombinant DNA   30

4 **DNA, Genes, and Protein**   48

5 **Engineering Plants**   68

6 **Genetically Modified Plants**
  From Herbicides to Vaccines   84

7 **Putting Genetically Modified**
  Organisms in Perspective   104

  Glossary   127
  Bibliography   133
  Further Reading   134
  Index   136

Introduction

By William G. Hopkins

"Have you thanked a green plant today?" reads a popular bumper sticker. Indeed we should thank green plants for providing the food we eat, fiber for the clothing we wear, wood for building our houses, and the oxygen we breathe. Without plants, humans and other animals simply could not exist. Psychologists tell us that plants also provide a sense of well-being and peace of mind, which is why we preserve forested parks in our cities, surround our homes with gardens, and install plants and flowers in our homes and workplaces. Gifts of flowers are the most popular way to acknowledge weddings, funerals, and other events of passage. Gardening is one of the fastest growing hobbies in North America and the production of ornamental plants contributes billions of dollars annually to the economy.

Human history has been strongly influenced by plants. The rise of agriculture in the fertile crescent of Mesopotamia brought previously scattered hunter-gatherers together into villages. Ever since, the availability of land and water for cultivating plants has been a major factor in determining the location of human settlements. World exploration and discovery was driven by the search for herbs and spices. The cultivation of new world crops—sugar, cotton, and tobacco—was responsible for the introduction of slavery to America, the human and social consequences of which are still with us. The push westward by English colonists into the rich lands of the Ohio River valley in the mid-1700s was driven by the need to increase corn production and was a factor in precipitating the French and Indian War. The Irish Potato Famine in 1847 set in motion a wave of migration, mostly to North America, that would reduce the population of Ireland by half over the next 50 years.

As a young university instructor directing biology tutorials in a classroom that looked out over a wooded area, I would ask each group of students to look out the window and tell me what they saw. More often than not the question would be met with a blank, questioning look. Plants are so much a part of our environment and the fabric of our everyday lives that they rarely register in our conscious thought. Yet today, faced with disappearing rainforests, exploding population growth, urban sprawl, and concerns about climate change, the productive capacity of global agricultural and forestry ecosystems is put under increasing pressure. Understanding plants is even more essential as we attempt to build a sustainable environment for the future.

The Green World series opens doors to the world of plants. The series describes what plants are, what plants do, and where plants fit into the overall scheme of things. *Plant Biotechnology* traces the development of biotechnology from prehistory to the present. It shows how plants are genetically engineered, weighs the risks and benefits of this new technology, and discusses the present impact and future potential of genetically modified plants.

1 What Is Biotechnology?

All problems are finally scientific problems.
—George Bernard Shaw (1856–1950)
Irish playwright

What Is Biotechnology?

It was late when he returned to the village. The moon had risen, and the other villagers were asleep in their huts. He had been hunting for meat and now he was hungry. Searching for something to eat, he spotted a bowl of grain that had been left sitting beside his hut for several days. It had rained recently and water had collected in the bowl. The grain was sprouting, but he took a handful anyway. It had an unfamiliar but pleasant taste, so he ate the rest of the grain and, to slake his thirst, he drank the liquor in which it had sat. As he sat resting by the remains of the cooking fire, he thought of the tales told by the elders in the village—tales of how their ancestors had moved constantly from place to place as they gathered the wild grains and of how there was never more than just enough to eat. He thought of how they now saved the fattest and healthiest of the grains and sowed them in the moist ground near the river so they no longer had to search for grain but simply waited for the crop to mature. They no longer had to move about, and there was always more than enough grain to feed the village. And as he sat and thought, he began to feel strange sensations. His vision began to blur and he felt dizzy. He thought, "I should go into the hut and sleep," but he had difficulty trying to rise and fell asleep where he sat.

BEER, CHEESE, AND FRESHLY BAKED BREAD

Is it possible that early man discovered beer in this way? Perhaps, but we don't really know, because the origins of brewing beer and other intoxicating beverages have been lost in antiquity. We do know that beer or a similar form of fermented beverage has been brewed and drunk by various civilizations for thousands of years. Archeological evidence tells us that as early as 11,000 years ago, there were agricultural villages established in the eastern Mediterranean area known as the Fertile Crescent, an area extending from the flood plains of the Tigris and Euphrates rivers in what is now Iraq, across Syria, and down the eastern coast of the Mediterranean to the Nile Valley of Egypt. Among the crops being domesticated were wheat and barley (used to produce beer) and grapes (for wine). It seems that bread-making and brewing were both early technologies associated with the beginnings of agriculture. It is known, for example, that the ancient Sumerians were producing a beer made from fermented, moistened bread more than 9,000 years ago. Wine, another fermented beverage, was also produced by the Sumerians as well as the ancient Egyptians.

The production of beer, wine, and bread involves the **fermentation** of the sugar glucose by a single-celled fungus called yeast, usually a strain of *Saccharomyces cerevisiae*. The yeast converts the glucose ($C_6H_{12}O_6$) to ethyl alcohol (ethanol, C_2H_5OH) and the gas carbon dioxide (CO_2):

$$C_6H_{12}O_6 \longrightarrow 2C_2H_5OH + 2CO_2$$

In the process of brewing beer, the germinating grain (usually barley) secretes an enzyme called amylase. The amylase acts on the starch in the endosperm (the nutritive tissue) of the seed, breaking down the starch into its component glucose, or sugar, units. The yeast that ferments the glucose is found naturally in the environment and, in the beginning at least, fermentation was the result of chance contamination. In other primitive societies, beerlike brews were made from other starchy plant products, and the amylase was often provided by chewing some of the plant material and spitting into the "brew." Amylase is a natural component of human saliva. Wine is a little easier to come by since the yeasts used to ferment the juices grow naturally on the surface of the fruit. The first wines would have been easily produced by simply allowing grape juices to stand for a few days.

Another early development was the production of cheese (Figure 1.1). Cheese, like wine, is a means for preserving food

Figure 1.1 A cheese maker stirs a cauldron of curd and the watery part of milk known as whey. Cheesemaking is one of the oldest examples of biotechnology.

and bears the same relationship to milk as wine does to grapes. The origin of cheese is equally obscure, although countless legends seem to involve a rider setting out on a horseback journey and carrying with him some milk in a pouch made from the stomach of a young cow. He later discovers, so the legend goes, that the milk has turned into a slightly sour mixture of watery fluid and curds. The reason, as we now know, is that the lining of a calf's stomach produces rennin, an enzyme that coagulates the milk proteins (albumin and casein). Cheese was well known to the Sumerians at least as far back as 6,000 years ago and has been made wherever domesticated animals produced more milk than could be immediately used by the people.

MAKING ORGANISMS WORK FOR US

What do beer, wine, bread, and cheese have to do with **biotechnology**, the topic of this book? The common thread is that all four involve harnessing living organisms or the products of living organisms to process food and make a specific product for humans.

Beer- and winemakers, of course, rely on the production of alcohol for their characteristic beverages. In early societies, there was probably little value, other than perhaps ceremonial, to the production of beerlike beverages. Wine production, on the other hand, has value as a means for preserving grapes or other fruits.

The breadmaker is not interested in alcohol production but takes advantage of the carbon dioxide gas to provide texture. When preparing bread, the dough is kneaded, which causes the flour proteins, called glutens, to form an elastic network. It is this gluten network that traps the carbon dioxide bubbles produced as the yeast ferments the glucose and maltose sugars present in the flour. When the dough has finally risen and is ready to bake, it also contains a significant amount of alcohol (as much as 0.5%), but this is driven off during baking and contributes to the enticing aroma that we associate with freshly baked bread.

Coagulation of milk proteins is a natural step in the digestion of milk by calves, young goats, and other young mammals. Humans have taken advantage of the enzymes involved to process and preserve the milk as food. Although rennin was formerly obtained from calf stomachs, worldwide cheese production has outstripped the supply of slaughtered calves. Fortunately, there are some fungi that produce extracellular (secreted into the organism's environment) enzymes, including rennin, that will coagulate milk. Fungi are now the principal commercial source of rennin for the cheese-making industry.

The use of living organisms to process foods and make other products that are useful to humans is what we generally refer to as "biotechnology." Because the word has only recently entered popular usage, most people think biotechnology is a very recent invention. The truth is that humans have been using other organisms to produce new products for a very long time. The first humans to discover bread, beer, wine, and cheese were, in fact, the world's first biotechnologists and we have been eating the products of biotechnology for thousands of years.

For most of history, biotechnology has focused on processing food for humans and cattle. The silage, or fodder, that becomes feed for livestock is stored by cattle and dairy farmers in silos and also is a fermented product. More recently, engineers have used fermentation to produce industrial **feedstocks** such as acetic acid and citric acid; drugs such as penicillin; ethanol for industrial purposes and as a gasoline additive; and to treat sewage. Engineers use the term *bioengineering* when engineering techniques are applied to biological processes, but for most of us the terms *bioengineering* and *biotechnology* are interchangeable and generally refer to any application of technology to living systems.

Over the past 30 years, biotechnology has come to mean something very different in the eyes of the general public. We hear about **genetic modification** (GM) and **genetically modified organisms** (GMOs), but we also hear about **genetic engineering** or **recombinant DNA** (rDNA). These new technologies have taken us far beyond just using biological fermentation to process foods, for we now have the ability to modify organisms at the most fundamental levels and make them work for us in ways previously undreamed of (Figure 1.2).

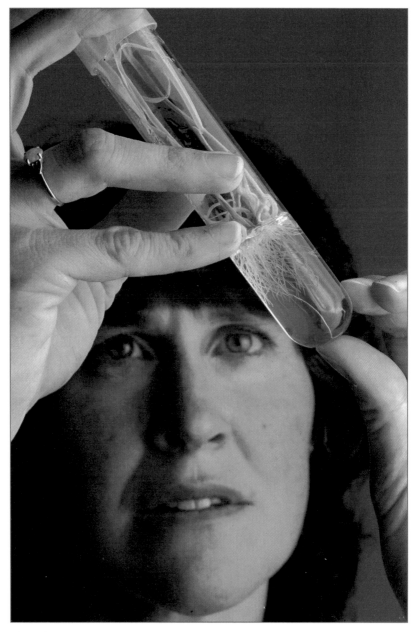

Figure 1.2 A scientist looks at root growth on wheat plants that have been genetically modified to resist infection by *Fusarium*, a type offungus. Scientists typically modify the genes of plants in order to increase yields or improve the nutritional quality of a plant.

This new biotechnology has unleashed a storm of public controversy. Proponents see the opportunity to help eradicate malnutrition, starvation, and genetic diseases. Opposition activists see scientists "playing God" and unleashing unspeakable monsters and ecological havoc. As with most new technologies, there is both benefit and risk involved with biotechnology and the truth will lie somewhere between these two extremes.

In the chapters that follow, we will trace the history of traditional biotechnology and how humans have manipulated microorganisms and plants over time. To help us better understand recombinant DNA technology, we will present an overview of

What's in a Word?

Even though the origins of biotechnology can be traced back thousands of years, it has only recently become part of the public consciousness. For example, in the *Webster's Encyclopedic Dictionary of the English Language* published in 1988, the word *biotechnology* is not listed. By that same year, however, the word *biotechnology* had already become well established as part of the dictionary of the scientific and academic world. The first genetically modified plant, a tobacco plant resistant to an antibiotic, had been created in 1983, and in 1986 the Environmental Protection Agency (EPA) approved the release of an herbicide-resistant tobacco variety. In 1988, the National Library of Medicine together with the National Institutes of Health (NIH) established the National Center for Biotechnology Information, with an emphasis, of course, on human and animal biotechnology.

Today, less than 20 years later, if you "google" *biotechnology*, you will bring up over 119 million "hits." There are thousands of biotechnology companies around the world, and most major universities have formal biotechnology courses or programs. A Google search for *plant biotechnology* alone will bring up over 15 million hits, and scarcely a day goes by that you cannot find a reference to biotechnology in major newspapers.

DNA and genes and look at how this new biotechnology came into being. We will show how plants are "genetically engineered" and how this new technology compares with traditional methods for producing new food plants. We will dispel some of the myths surrounding genetic modification and review the present impact and future potential of genetically modified plants. In the final chapter, we will examine some of the moral and ethical questions surrounding genetically modified organisms.

Summary

The discoveries of the fermentation process to make beer and wine and the use of enzymes from animals to make cheese are all lost in antiquity, but they harness the activities of living organisms. Using living organisms to process foods and to manufacture other products that are useful to humankind is commonly referred to as "biotechnology." Beginning in the 1980s, however, the word *biotechnology* has taken on a whole new meaning. Most people now understand the term *biotechnology* to mean the manipulation of an organism's genes to create genetically modified organisms (GMOs). This book will trace the development of biotechnology from its early beginnings to the present, explain the science behind biotechnology, and help the reader make an informed judgment about the role of biotechnology in the future.

2 The Early Days of Biotechnology

There are science and the applications of science, linked together as fruit to the tree that has borne it.

—Louis Pasteur (1822–1895)
French chemist and microbiologist

The Early Days of Biotechnology

SCIENTIFIC ROOTS OF BIOTECHNOLOGY

The origins of biotechnology as a science can be traced back to 1857, when French biologist Louis Pasteur (1822–1895) discovered that the fermentation of lactic acid was due to the action of live microbes, or microorganisms (Figure 2.1). Pasteur's discovery not only gave rise to the science of microbiology and contributed to the salvation of the French silk and wine industry, but it also stimulated a general interest in brewing and other types of industrial fermentation. Fermentation on an industrial scale grew during the latter half of the nineteenth century and was used to produce a number of important commercial products. The industry represented a marriage of microbiology with chemical engineering that became known as zymotechnology (from *zymology*, the scientific study of fermentation). The term *zymotechnology* has since been replaced with the more encompassing term *biotechnology*.

The first recorded use of the term *biotechnology* is credited to a Hungarian agricultural engineer, Karl Ereky, nearly 100 years ago. In an effort to modernize Hungarian agriculture in the early years of the twentieth century, Ereky sought and obtained funding to support agriculture on an industrial scale. In 1919, Ereky published a tract with the German title *Biotechnologie der Fleisch-, Fett-, und Milcherzeugung im Landwirtschaftlichen Großbetriebe* ("Biotechnology of Meat, Fat, and Milk Production in Large-scale Agricultural Industry"). Ereky's enterprise became one of the world's largest and most productive meat operations. His farm covered 50 hectares (110 acres) and turned out over 100,000 pigs a year. We tend to treat "factory farms" as a recent North American innovation, but large-scale farms, especially for pigs, were common in Germany and eastern Europe in the early twentieth century.

Two manufacturing processes illustrate the "state of the art" of biotechnology shortly after the turn of the twentieth century. In 1911, German scientist C. A. Neuberg showed that significant

Figure 2.1 Louis Pasteur was a pioneer in the field of biotechnology. He is perhaps best known for inventing pasteurization, which is the process of heating a beverage or other food in order to destroy harmful microorgansims.

amounts of glycerol could be produced by fermentation of starch. Four years later, German industry was able to produce more than 12,000 tonnes (a tonne is a metric ton = 1,000 kilograms or 2,200 pounds) of glycerol per year.

At the same time in Britain, a group of organic chemists at Manchester University began working on the rubber problem. At that time, Brazil held a monopoly on "wild" rubber trees, although British plantations were being established in Malaysia. With the rise of the automobile industry, a reliable supply of rubber was becoming increasingly important. In order to break the Brazilian monopoly on rubber, however, the world needed a good synthetic rubber. The Manchester University group included a young Russian immigrant, Chaim Weizmann (who would later become the first president of the state of Israel). In 1912, Weizmann was instrumental in developing a fermentation method to produce **butanol**. Butanol was readily converted to butadiene, the raw material for producing a superior synthetic butyl rubber.

Fortuitously, a second product of the so-called Weizmann process was acetone. Acetone was another commercially important chemical as an ingredient in the manufacture of explosives. In addition, acetone and butanol together could be used to make isobutyl acetate, the best solvent known for the new plastic nitrocellulose. Interestingly, nitrocellulose was the film on which the early stars of Hollywood were immortalized. Nitrocellulose was also the source of gun cotton, a component of high explosives. (Yes, the early films produced by Hollywood were highly flammable!)

And what about all that glycerol being produced by fermentation in Germany at the same time? When glycerol is chemically reacted with nitric acid, the product is nitroglycerin. Nitroglycerin, which is extremely unstable and highly explosive, was the explosive of choice for early miners. In 1867, Swedish inventor Alfred Nobel discovered that the explosive power of nitroglycerin could be stabilized by absorbing the liquid on an inert (non-reactive) powder, thus producing dynamite. Dynamite made Nobel a very rich man and, on his death, he endowed the international prizes that bear his name. Rubber and explosives—it is not difficult to draw connections between the direction taken by biotechnology in the years prior to 1918 and the developing political climate of the time, which culminated in World War I.

The Weizmann process proved to be significant in many ways, not just for its economic impact. Most industrial fermentations up to then were carried out in oak casks—continuing in the brewing tradition, of course—and did not require **aseptic** (sterile) conditions. The Weizmann process, on the other hand, required that laboratory standards for sterility be maintained on an industrial scale and production was carried out in modern aluminum fermentation vessels. Weizmann's process sealed a partnership between microbiology, chemical engineering, and modern materials that was to dominate biotechnology until the 1980s, when recombinant DNA came on the scene.

WHAT IS FERMENTATION?

One of the more interesting things about nature is its extreme conservatism. In spite of their striking differences, organisms as diverse as fungi, oak trees, earthworms, and elephants all share many of the same genes and do things, in a metabolic sense at least, in much the same way. For example, when organisms break down sugars, fats, and proteins to retrieve energy, the pathway used is virtually identical in all living organisms. The end result, however, is different depending on whether or not oxygen is available. When oxygen is present, this pathway is called **cellular respiration**. When oxygen is absent, the same pathway is called **fermentation**.

The initial steps of respiration and fermentation, a process called **glycolysis**, are the same. In preparation for respiration or fermentation, complex storage molecules such as starch (plants) or glycogen (animals) must first be broken down into their component glucose molecules. Glucose, a simple sugar made up of six carbon atoms, is further broken down through glycolysis (Figure 2.2). The net result of glycolysis is that one six-carbon molecule (glucose) is converted to two three-carbon molecules called

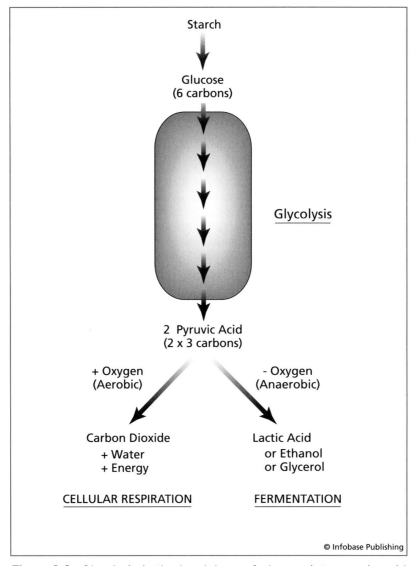

Starch

Glucose
(6 carbons)

Glycolysis

2 Pyruvic Acid
(2 x 3 carbons)

+ Oxygen
(Aerobic)

- Oxygen
(Anaerobic)

Carbon Dioxide
+ Water
+ Energy

Lactic Acid
or Ethanol
or Glycerol

CELLULAR RESPIRATION

FERMENTATION

© Infobase Publishing

Figure 2.2 Glycolysis is the breakdown of glucose into pyruvic acid inside cells. The pyruvic acid molecules are broken down further via two different pathways depending on the presence or absence of oxygen.

pyruvic acid. A small amount of energy is released, and the carbon atoms in the glucose have been slightly rearranged, but otherwise not a lot has happened up to this point.

The difference between respiration and fermentation lies in the fate of pyruvic acid. When oxygen is present, the pyruvic acid enters a metabolic pathway called the citric acid cycle (or Krebs cycle), where it is completely broken down into carbon dioxide and most of the energy is retrieved for use by the cell. This is what normally happens in your own cells to provide the energy the cells need to function. In the absence of oxygen, however, the citric acid cycle shuts down and the pyruvate undergoes more limited changes. This is what we call fermentation. Depending on the organism and the conditions of fermentation, a variety of end products are possible.

> • **Lactic acid:** The fermentation product in human muscle when exercising under oxygen debt. Lactic acid is responsible for muscle soreness, and it is also the fermentation product of certain fungi and bacteria. Lactic acid can be converted to iso-prene, which can be used in the manufacture of synthetic butyl rubber.

> • **Ethyl alcohol (ethanol):** The fermentation product of several fungi, especially *Saccharomyces cerevisiae.*

> • **Glycerol:** Under alkaline conditions, *S. cerevisiae* produces glycerol instead of ethanol.

> • **Acetic acid (vinegar):** The fermentation product of the bacterium *Acetobacter*. Contamination of wine with *Acetobacter* can be a problem for wine producers because the acetic acid sours the wine. Acetic acid is widely used as a raw material in the manufacture of fibers, plastics, and other industrial products.

PROCESSING FOOD AND DRINK

In modern systems of classification, fungi are no longer considered plants, but since the beginnings of biotechnology are so intimately associated with the fungi, we will consider them as close cousins to the plants and include them in our discussions. In addition to beer, wine, and bread, fungi are used in the processing of many different foods, especially in Asia. As with beer and wine, the fungi are used to improve the texture, flavor, and nutritional value of foods as well as to delay spoilage.

In Japan, China, and other Asian countries, a large variety of foods are prepared from soybeans (*Glycine max*). These include tempeh, a solid food prepared by processing soybeans with the fungus *Rhizopus* species; sufu, a Chinese cheese prepared from soybeans with the help of the fungus *Actinomucor elegans*; and soy sauce, a condiment prepared by fermenting soybeans and wheat with *Aspergillus oryzae*.

In addition to fungi, bacteria have also proven useful in traditional biotechnology. As noted earlier, bacteria produce acetic acid, which is used in preserving and flavoring foods and as an important industrial feedstock. In Europe and North America, lactic acid produced by the bacterium *Lactobacillus* has long been used to preserve cabbage (sauerkraut) and naturally fermented pickles.

INDUSTRIAL PRODUCTION OF FUNGAL METABOLITES

We have seen how fungi have been used to process foods, changing both the flavor and the composition of foodstuffs. Fungi also produce a wide range of **metabolites,** or chemical products of metabolism, that have commercial use on their own. These products include organic acids, alcohols, antibiotics, vitamins, and enzymes (Table 2.1). In almost all cases, modern industrial fermentation methods have made it possible to produce these products in larger amounts, higher purity, and more often at lower cost than by direct chemical synthesis.

Large-scale production of chemicals by fungi is usually carried out in vats or tanks with a capacity of several thousand liters. The vat is filled with a watery solution of some carbon source, such as cane syrup or molasses, and supplemented with vitamins and amino acids to ensure rapid, healthy growth of the microorganisms. The tank is then inoculated with the appropriate organism. The tank may be aerated, if the culture requires oxygen, or sealed if anaerobic conditions are required. Either way, actively growing organisms release a lot of heat, so the culture will be cooled by circulating water through coils surrounding the tank. Once the culture has run its course, the cells are separated from the culture medium and the metabolite of interest is extracted by filtration and chemical extraction. The culture tanks are often cylindrical and, with various filters, pumps, and cooling coils, the entire set-up may resemble a miniature oil refinery. Commercial production may involve either **batch culture**, in which the vat is emptied after the reaction runs its course, or **continuous culture**, in which the culture medium flows through the tank and production of the desired metabolite continues indefinitely. We will have more to say about the continuous culture method later.

Table 2.1   Commercially Important Fungal Metabolites Produced by Biotechnology

Metabolite	Use
Organic Acids	
Citric acid	Flavoring ingredient in candies, soft drinks, medicines; used in inks and the dye industry
Alcohols	
Ethyl alcohol	Industrial solvent, medicines, raw material in the manufacture of materials such as ether, acetic acid, synthetic rubber
Glycerol	Glycerin; explosives
Drugs	
Penicillin	Oral and injectible antibiotic
Griseofulvin	Oral and topical antibiotic

(continued on page 22)

(continued from page 21)

Metabolite	**Use**
Vitamins and Growth Factors	
B vitamins	Nutritional supplement and medical therapy
Riboflavin	Nutritional supplement and medical therapy
Gibberellin	Plant growth hormone with commercial applications in floricultural
Beta-carotene	Synthesis of vitamin A (provitamin A), nutritional supplement, and coloring agent for margarine
Enzymes	
Amylase	Conversion of starch to sugars prior to fermentation
Rennet	Milk coagulation in the manufacture of cheese
Invertase	Hydrolyzes sucrose (table sugar) to glucose and fructose
Pectinase	Pretreatment of fruit juices to remove turbidity; removal of pectins before concentrating fruit juices
Proteases	Hydrolysis of proteins during food processing

One of the most important organic acids produced commercially from large-scale fungal cultures is citric acid. It is used as a flavoring in beverages and foods (especially gelatin powders and soft-drink crystals), desserts, jellies, candies, and frozen fruits. Citric acid is widely used in pharmaceuticals, **effervescent** products, and blood transfusions. It is used in hair rinses, electroplating, and leather tanning. Citric acid was originally obtained from lemons, but now virtually all of it is produced industrially by the fungus *Aspergillus niger*. Annual production worldwide exceeds several hundred million kilograms (1 kg = 2.2 pounds).

Still, the largest and most important products of commercial bioengineering are antibiotics, especially penicillin. Penicillin was discovered in 1929 when Alexander Fleming (1881–1955) observed that his cultures of a pathogenic (disease-causing) bacterium, *Staphylococcus aureus,* had been contaminated by a mold. The mold, growing in a petri dish, was surrounded by a clear ring where it had killed the bacteria in its immediate vicinity. The contaminating fungus was identified as a species of *Penicillium,* so the active principal was called penicillin. Although penicillin was recognized as an effective antibiotic, it found little use because its production was difficult and yields were low. The increased need for effective antibiotics as a result of World War II stimulated the search for efficient methods for large-scale production.

Penicillin is produced commercially using strains of *Penicillium chrysogenum* cultured on a medium such as corn steep liquor, a by-product of corn starch manufacturing. Corn steep liquor is a concentrate of water-soluble materials from the corn grain and is especially rich in nitrogen-containing chemicals that are necessary for a good yield of the antibiotic. The corn steep liquor is inoculated with the fungus and incubated for five or six days, after which the fungus is filtered off and the penicillin is chemically extracted and purified from the liquor that remains.

A third example of industrial bioengineering is the production of ethanol. Ethyl alcohol production as an end product of anaerobic fermentation in beer and wine production is, as we have seen, the oldest form of biotechnology. Ethanol also has many industrial uses as a solvent and, more recently, as a biofuel. In the early part of the twentieth century, as much as 75% of the industrial ethanol production was achieved by fermentation and subsequent distillation of molasses, but molasses is comparatively expensive and occasionally in short supply. It became cheaper to produce ethanol from petroleum, which at the time appeared to be relatively inexpensive and abundant. Now, with increasing concerns about diminishing oil supplies and a focus on renewable resources, attention has once more turned to fermentation as a source of industrial ethanol.

Brazil has led the way in ethanol production because it has abundant supplies of cane sugar, which is readily fermented. In North America, the favored substrate (material being fermented) is corn starch, but the starch must first be treated with enzymes that break the starch into soluble sugars. Yeasts can then ferment the soluble sugars into ethanol. Other potential sources of carbohydrate for ethanol production include starches and sugars of sweet potatoes and the cellulose that makes up wheat straw. These too must be treated with enzymes before beginning the fermentation process.

Bacteria and fungi are also the source of numerous enzymes that have commercial application. We have already mentioned rennin, used in the production of cheese. Protein-degrading enzymes such as papain are used to clarify beer. Glucose isomerase is an example of an enzyme that has given rise to a major industry. When starch is broken down completely, the product is the 6-carbon sugar glucose. Glucose isomerase is the enzyme that plants and many other organisms use to convert glucose to another 6-carbon sugar called **fructose**. Beginning in the 1960s, high-fructose corn syrups derived from corn starch have completely replaced cane sugar (sucrose) in soft drinks. High-fructose syrups are also used extensively in the baking, canning, and food-preserving industries. The reason that high-fructose syrups are so popular is that fructose is twice as sweet as conventional sugar (sucrose, or table sugar). The high sweetness of fructose means that much less sugar—and therefore fewer calories—is required.

The industrial use of enzymes again illustrates the synergies between biotechnology and chemical engineering. Enzymes are expensive to produce and use. To perform enzyme conversions by batch culture can be inefficient and costly. Because enzymes are organic catalysts, organisms do not need to make large quantities of them. Instead, they use the same enzyme over and over again in

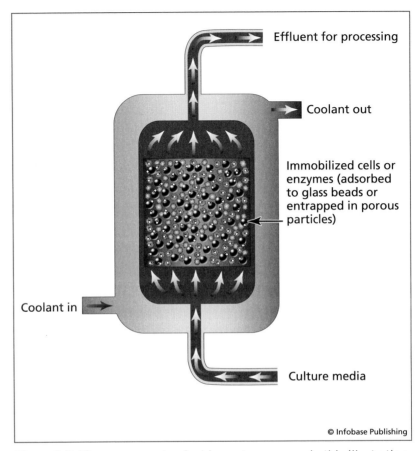

Figure 2.3 The components of a bioreactor are seen in this illustration. A bioreactor is a vessel in which microorganisms, cells, or enzymes are used to break down harmful substances or create useful products.

order to produce large amounts of product. In the early 1960s, it was found that industry could follow the same strategy. Enzymes such as glucose isomerase are now sealed to the surface of an inert bed, such as glass beads or cellulose, to form a **bioreactor**. Fructose is then produced continuously simply by passing a stream of glucose solution through the reactor. This flow-through process continually renews the supply of substrate processed by the same enzymes and the reactor produces a continuous stream of effluent that is rich in fructose (Figure 2.3).

WASTE MANAGEMENT AND BIOREMEDIATION

One area where traditional biotechnology has proven particularly effective is in waste management and remediation of waste water. Home and municipal septic systems are the classic example, where bacteria have long been used to degrade solid wastes. Small-scale pilot projects have also demonstrated that plants can also play a role in sewage management. After a primary treatment in a septic tank, the effluent enters an artificial "wetland" planted with a mixture of sedges (*Carex* spp.), reeds (*Phragmites* spp.), bulrushes (*Juncus* spp.), and cattails (*Typha* spp.). The wetland provides for additional purification of the wastewater by aerobic bacteria. The plants serve two primary functions: they hold the bacteria in place and, through the process of transpiration, maximize the evaporation of water into the atmosphere. If the effluent contains heavy metals, these may also be removed by plants that grow in the artificial wetland. We will return to this interesting property of plants in chapter 3.

Bacteria are now being used extensively to treat industrial wastes other than sewage and to clean up contaminated groundwater. The use of living organisms such as bacteria to clean up environmental sites contaminated with chemical pollutants is known as **bioremediation** (*bio* meaning "living" and *remediation* meaning "to correct a fault"). The systems used are generally like that described above for enzymes. The bacteria are cultivated on an inert bed (activated carbon is commonly used) in a cylindrical reactor chamber and the water to be treated is pumped through from the bottom. The contaminant is broken down by the bacteria as it passes through the reactor and purified water comes out the other end. This kind of system is now being used with denitrifying bacteria for removal of nitrates from industrial and municipal wastewater and for remediation of contaminated groundwater.

Other areas where this general approach has proven beneficial include decontamination of soils at decommissioned oil refineries and removal of perchlorate from groundwater. The latter is a particularly serious problem in California, Utah, Nevada, and Texas, where ammonium perchlorate (NH_4ClO_4) was used for decades as an oxidizing agent in solid propellants and explosives. Discharge from manufacturing operations and from replacement of outdated fuels in military missiles and rockets was and remains a major source of groundwater contamination. Bacteria are now being used extensively to clean up the groundwater by breaking the perchlorate down into harmless chloride and water. Similar innovative strategies are being used to clean up a wide range of toxic chemicals in various environmental situations (Figure 2.4). Different strains of bacteria such

Bioreactors

A term that has begun to permeate the bioengineering field is *bioreactor*, used broadly to indicate any vessel or container where organisms are used to produce a product. The organism may be microorganisms, plant cells, or animal cells. In that sense, fermentation vats used to produce citric acid or penicillin would be considered bioreactors. Indeed, an entire industry has developed around the design and manufacture of bioreactors using batch culture or immobilized cells for the production of enzymes, vaccines, hormones, pharmaceuticals, and a host of other useful chemicals. Most bioreactors consist of tanks surrounded by pumps and pipes that move fluids and gases into the reaction chamber, provide cooling, and remove effluent for downstream chemical processing. Bioreactors may range in size from small, bench-top devices for laboratory experimentation and testing up to large industrial versions that process several thousand liters. The concept of bioreactor has even been extended to include the use of bacteria to assist in the breakdown of materials deposited into landfills and the use of genetically modified plants to produce chemicals with industrial or pharmaceutical value.

as *Pseudomonas* and *Escherichia coli* are capable of degrading hundreds of different toxic chemicals.

Soils near oil refineries are often contaminated with **hydrocarbons**, such as unrefined petroleum oil, diesel fuel, or gasoline. In one such situation, several bioreactors were used to decontaminate the soil around a decommissioned refinery near Lake Ontario, where an area covering 15 acres was contaminated with hydrocarbons to a depth of three feet. Nutrients were supplied to encourage the growth of microorganisms already present in the soil, and within two years the hydrocarbon levels were reduced by 97%.

Finally, one of the most well-known examples of bacteria in bioremediation efforts is the follow-up of the Exxon *Valdez* oil spill in Prince William Sound off the coast of Alaska in 1989. Initially, physical cleaning measures, such a steam cleaning and rinsing, were put in place to contain and remove large volumes of oil. The beaches were then treated with nitrogen and phosphorus fertilizers to accelerate the growth of oil-degrading bacteria that lived among the rocks and sand. Although the process is not yet complete, careful monitoring of the site has shown that the bacteria have degraded a significant amount of the oil and have even restored some sections of the shoreline to pre-spill conditions.

Summary

The origins of biotechnology as a science can be traced back to Pasteur's discovery that fermentation was caused by microorganisms. This stimulated the development of fermentation on an industrial scale to produce a variety of feed stocks that supplied the manufacturing industry. The term *biotechnology* was first used by Karl Ereky in the early twentieth century in the context of large-scale agricultural meat and milk production. In addition to producing products for the manufacturing

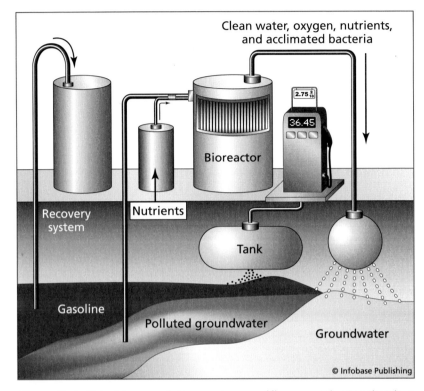

Figure 2.4 This bioremediation system purifies groundwater that has been contaminated with gasoline. The polluted groundwater is pumped into a bioreactor that contains oxygen, nutrients, and bacteria. The microbes degrade the gasoline and the clean water is then pumped back into the ground.

industry, biotechnology and bioengineering have been used throughout the twentieth century to produce drugs such as penicillin, process food and drink, control waste management, and clean up contaminated soils.

3 Plants and Biotechnology
Before Recombinant DNA

30

Any sufficiently advanced technology is indistinguishable from magic.
—Arthur C. Clarke (1917–)
British author and inventor

Plants and Biotechnology
Before Recombinant DNA

Traditional biotechnology has not been limited to applications involving microorganisms. Even before genetic modification arrived on the scene, plants had been enlisted to serve human needs in a variety of ways beyond their traditional role of providing food and fiber.

PHYTOREMEDIATION: CLEANING UP WITH PLANTS

Have you ever heard of locoweed? As a child, I watched a lot of B-grade movie Westerns and one thing I learned was that, if you are a rancher, you don't want your cattle grazing on locoweed! Locoweed is the common name given to several species of *Astragalus*, a genus in the Fabaceae or pea family. Also known as milk vetch or poison vetch, many species of *Astragalus* take up unusually large quantities of selenium from the alkaline soils of the western plains. The high selenium content contributes to a disease known as alkali poisoning or "blind staggers" in cattle unfortunate enough to graze on this plant—the cattle literally behave as though they are crazy.

There are many regions where natural geochemical processes have produced soils that are rich in metals such as nickel, chromium, gold, cadmium, selenium, and arsenic. Normally high levels of heavy metals would be toxic to plants, just as they are to humans, yet many plants actually thrive on soils rich in such metals. For some plants, the metals are not a problem simply because the cell membranes surrounding the root cells prevent the metals from entering the root. Other plants actually take up the metals and accumulate them to levels that would be toxic to most other plants (Figure 3.1). In *Astragalus*, for example, selenium may account for as much as 10% of the dry weight of the seeds. In soils that are rich in nickel, some plants may contain 200,000 times more nickel than plants growing in normal soils.

Many years ago, such plants were known as "indicator species," and prospectors would take the presence of such plants as an early indication that the soils may have contained a mineral of interest, such as gold. This was called **phytoprospecting**. We now call these

Figure 3.1 An agronomist examines the roots of a *Thlaspi* plant in a growth chamber. *Thlaspi* and other metal-accumulating plants can be used to remove heavy metal contamination from soils.

plants **accumulator species,** which are not injured by high concentrations of heavy metals because they **sequester** (isolate) the metals with small proteins called **phytochelatins.** The sequestered metals are then stored in the large central vacuole of the plant cell, where they cannot interfere with the cell's metabolism.

There has recently been a renewed interest in accumulator species because these plants may have the potential to assist in cleaning up soils contaminated with heavy metals as a result of twentieth-century industrial activities. Using plants to clean up soils is called **phytoremediation** (*phyto* meaning "plant" and *remediation* meaning "to correct a fault"). The idea is to grow accumulator species on mine tailings and wastes from paper mills, for example, where they would extract the heavy metals. Plants will naturally take longer to do the job, but plants are much more cost-effective and would not create even more ecological problems as engineering-based technologies often do. Phytoremediation would also help to stabilize contaminated sites because the plants help to control erosion.

An additional benefit of accumulator species is that they begin the revegetation of barren industrial sites and assist in the recovery of useful metals. Phytomining, as it is called, has proven effective in the recovery of both nickel and thallium in demonstrations. In

Selenium and Alkali Poisoning

It is interesting that selenium would poison cattle because selenium is actually an essential trace mineral for mammalian metabolism and is widely incorporated into cattle feed. This is because selenium is part of a twenty-first amino acid. All the textbooks will tell you that proteins are synthesized from twenty "standard" amino acids specified by the "standard" genetic code. But several enzymes require a twenty-first amino acid called seleno-cysteine which, of course, contains selenium. It is often the case, however, that trace elements (those required by organisms in very small amounts) become toxic when there is too much available. Plants, for example, require several trace elements, including boron, zinc, manganese, copper, nickel, and molybdenum. Most trace elements serve necessary functions as enzyme cofactors, non-protein molecules that must be present for an enzyme to function. Although plants require very small amounts of these trace elements in order to function properly, any one of them can become toxic at relatively low concentrations.

other trials, various species of willows (*Salix*) have shown promise for extraction of heavy metals from soils treated with sewage sludge. The advantage of using plants is that they can be harvested and burned. The heavy metals remain concentrated in the ash, which makes their disposal much easier.

MICROPROPAGATION: STARTING OUT SMALL

Cloning is one of the buzzwords of the new biotechnology (not to mention medical mystery stories and science fiction), but gardeners, farmers, and plant scientists have been cloning plants long before the first cloned sheep, Dolly, arrived on the scene in 1996. A clone can be defined as a genetically uniform assemblage of individuals derived originally from a single organism by asexual reproduction. That may sound just a bit imposing, but the two keys concepts here are "genetically uniform" and "asexual reproduction." All organisms contain at least two copies, called **alleles**, for every gene. During sexual reproduction—by seed, for example—the alleles from each parent are randomly reassorted when they are passed to the offspring. The result is that, except in the case of identical twins in mammals, no two offspring resulting from sexual reproduction have exactly the same genetic constitution. The offspring are not genetically uniform. Genetic reassortment is a distinct advantage in the natural world because it is the only way to ensure that at least some of the offspring have the genetic constitution to be more competitive when meeting new challenges in the environment.

In the world of horticulture and agriculture, however, there is profit to be had in genetically uniform lines that exhibit a particular trait or traits. It may be size, flower color, yield, or some other marketable characteristic. It is an advantage for the producer to be able to provide uniform plants on a predictable basis and that is possible only if the genetic makeup of the plants can be maintained without change from one generation to the next. The only way to maintain a line of genetically uniform individuals, or clones, is to resort to asexual reproduction. In plants, asexual or **vegetative reproduction,** is very common. One often sees "clumps" or small groups of poplar trees, for example, that are in fact a single tree. Each individual arises as an **adventitious shoot** from the roots of an original tree that may have started from seed. Each tree in the group is therefore a genetically identical clone.

Gardeners and plant breeders routinely reproduce plants vegetatively by simply making cuttings, inducing the cuttings to form roots, and planting them. Another common method for vegetative reproduction is a form of biotechnology called **micropropagation**, which uses plant tissue culture (Figure 3.2). Today, micropropagation is a multimillion-dollar business. Many common houseplants, fruit trees, and forest trees began life in a test tube or petri dish. By the early 1980s, growers in the Netherlands alone were producing over 21 million plants annually by micropropagation.

Some 70 years ago, Phillip White gave birth to the science of plant tissue culture when he successfully maintained cut tomato roots in vitro. *In vitro* means literally "in glass," but the expression refers to the culture of organisms in test tubes, petri dishes, or other laboratory glassware. In tissue culture, a small piece of plant is cut out and placed into **aseptic**, or bacteria-free, culture on a synthetic medium in a flask or petri dish. The medium usually contains agar, a semisolid gel obtained from certain species of algae, supplemented with sucrose as a carbon source plus some vitamins, essential minerals, and hormones. Under these conditions, the cells begin to divide and grow and form a clump of undifferentiated cells called a callus. By adjusting the culture conditions, often by modifying the hormone balance, it is possible to stimulate the callus to form plantlets with roots and shoots. Once the roots and shoots are established, these plantlets can be removed from the flask and planted in the greenhouse, where they will continue to grow, flower, set seed, and do all the other things that plants normally do.

Figure 3.2 A plant biologist examines papaya plantlets raised in a petri dish by micropropagation. The plantlets will undergo further testing to see whether they will yield flowers, which will then develop into fruit.

All this is made possible by the fact that virtually every plant cell is **totipotent**—it has the genetic potential to reproduce the entire organism. All one has to do to make use of this potential is to find the conditions that allow the potential to be expressed. Even cells that have matured and already assumed specific functions can be made to reverse the differentiation process and differentiate along a different developmental path. Unlike plant cells, animal cells are not generally totipotent: Most animal cells become highly differentiated early in their development and this differentiation cannot be reversed. The major exception is animal stem cells, which retain some capacity to differentiate down different paths. But even stem cells are not capable of producing an entire animal.

The most important commercial technique for micropropagating plants is known as **shoot-tip culture** (Table 3.1). One simply cuts out a small tip of a shoot (called the explant) that includes the growing region of the shoot (the **apical meristem**) and a few of the most recently formed leaves. This explant may be as little as 2–3 millimeters long. The explant is first washed with a dilute solution of household bleach to remove any contaminating fungi or bacteria. It is then placed on the culture medium under sterile conditions. The shoot tip will continue to grow and, as it grows, numerous **microshoots** will appear. Microshoots arise from small groups of dividing cells that remain trapped where the young leaves join the stem. These are called axillary buds. This is the same

Table 3.1   Crops Commonly Propagated by Shoot-tip Culture

Apple (*Malus*)	Peach, Cherry (*Prunus*)
Carnation (*Dianthus*)	Poplar (*Populus*)
Chrysanthemum	Rhododendron
Grape (*Vitis*)	(*Rhododendron*)
Kiwi fruit (*Actinidia*)	Rose (*Rosa*)
Orchids (*Cattleya, Cymbidium*)	Strawberry (*Fragaria*)

thing that happens on a much larger scale when gardeners prune plants in order to encourage the proliferation of axillary or lateral shoots and produce bushier plants.

After two to four weeks, the mass of shoots is divided and the pieces are transferred to fresh culture medium. This process is repeated, and each time the cluster of shoots is divided and subcultured, the number of microshoots increases exponentially. Through shoot-tip culture, literally millions of genetically identical microshoots can be cloned from a single desirable parent. When a sufficient number of microshoots have been generated, they are transferred to a medium with an appropriate hormone balance that stimulates root formation. The young plantlets can then be planted in the greenhouse and grown to maturity.

There are a number of advantages to micropropagation over traditional methods of plant propagation. One is that exceptionally large numbers of seedlings can be produced in a very small amount of space. In the floral industry, it is commonly used to produce clones of cultivars (varieties under cultivation) that are particularly popular because of flower color or other characteristics. The technique is used extensively in the production of forest tree species for planting in tree plantations and reforestation efforts because it avoids the tedious process of collecting and germinating seeds. Moreover, trees with superior characteristics can be cloned for higher productivity. On the other hand, cloning trees for commercial pulp and logging industries does reduce the genetic diversity of the forest, which could have long-term detrimental effects. Genetic diversity enables some members of a population to survive stresses that might damage others. In a cloned forest, however, if the clone turns out to be particularly susceptible to drought or a new disease, the entire forest is at risk.

Micropropagation is also an effective way to eliminate viruses and other pathogens. In fact, the first plants to be mass-produced by micropropagation were virus-free clones of *Cymbidium* orchids. Potato is another plant that is often troubled with virus infections. Potatoes are normally propagated vegetatively by buds, or "eyes," on the tubers, and any virus infection is readily carried from one generation to the next. The most effective way to eliminate potato viruses is by micropropagation of virus-free lines through shoot-tip cultures.

Micropropagation, like any other technique, is not perfect but is subject to the whims of nature. In spite of the fact that clones are supposed to be identical, significant variations can sometimes arise. These variations, which probably involve spontaneous mutations due to the culture conditions, are known as **somaclonal variations.** Most somaclonal variants are discarded, but occasionally one exhibits a particularly useful trait relating to field crops or an interesting flower color, so all is not lost. The use of somaclonal variation as a plant breeding technique is described in chapter 7.

BIOFUELS

It may sound like the stuff of folklore, but if you should happen to live near a swamp, you may occasionally have seen fires dancing across the surface of the swamp. What actually causes these fires is methane gas (CH_4). In stagnant swamps, any dissolved oxygen is used up rather quickly and, since there is no significant mixing of water and air, there is little opportunity for the oxygen supply to be replenished. Under these conditions, anaerobic bacteria, which thrive in the absence of oxygen, will take over. Anaerobic bacteria break down the organic material in the swamp and, in the process, generate methane gas. Methane is commonly known as marsh gas or swamp gas. It is also the principal constituent of natural gas, which is usually found in association with petroleum deposits.

There are many sources of methane in addition to swamps and petroleum deposits. The principal sources today are cattle flatulence, municipal sewage treatment plants, and landfill sites. We can't do much about the cattle, but most landfill sites, particularly in urban areas where they have been reclaimed for parks or housing, are now vented by driving pipes through the soil cover into the landfill. The pipes allow the methane to escape into the atmosphere rather than accumulate in the landfill where it poses a danger to human health. More recently, we have come to recognize that this methane represents a potential energy source and the amount of gas that can be generated in landfills is significant. Consequently, landfills are now being engineered as giant bioreactors to capture the methane gas for use as a fuel. Methane generated under these circumstances is commonly referred to as **biogas**. Methane is commonly produced on farms in areas such as silos and manure storage tanks. It can become a real hazard, as every year numerous farm workers are killed when overcome by gases, including methane. Many farmers are now designing bioreactors in order to recover biogas from agricultural wastes for use as an on-farm source of energy.

Another source of biofuel that is gaining in popularity is the oil that many plants store in their seeds. The energy content of most plant oils compares favorably to that of petroleum-based diesel fuel. The energy content of sunflower oil, for example, is 37 megajoules (MJ) per kilogram compared with 42 MJ in a kilogram of crude oil. Known as biodiesel, some plant oils can be used directly in farm machinery and other diesel engines. Most plant oils, however, are **triglycerides**. A triglyceride is a fat or oil molecule that has three long carbon chains, called **fatty acids**, attached to a 3-carbon molecule called glycerol (or glycerin) (Figure 3.3). It won't do you much good to simply pour triglycerides into your tank because the oils would clog up the fuel injectors and could cause permanent damage to the engine. Before they can be used as a fuel, triglycerides must first be processed, which involves separating the fatty acids from the glycerol. Once the glycerol is removed, the free fatty acids may be used in place of ordinary petrochemical-based diesel fuel.

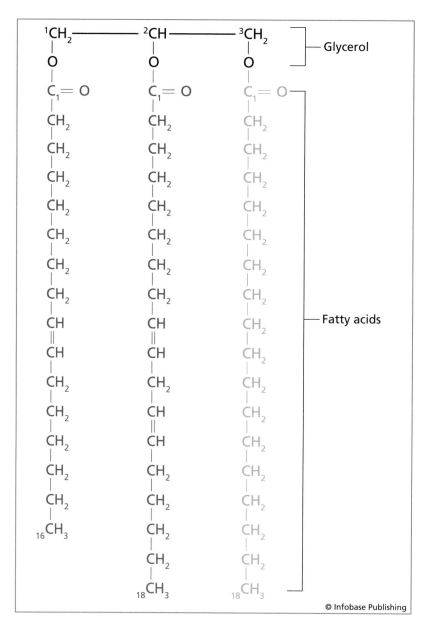

Figure 3.3 A triglyceride consists of three fatty acids attached to a glycerol molecule. Fatty acids in which all the carbon atoms are joined by single bonds are said to be saturated (such as the green fatty acid in illustration). Fatty acids with one or more double bonds between carbon atoms are classified as unsaturated (red and blue in illustration).

Although diesel engines can run on pure processed vegetable oil, it is usually mixed with regular diesel fuel to improve combustion and performance. According to the U.S. Department of Energy, more than 25 million gallons of biodiesel were produced in 2004 and production in 2005 was expected to approach 100 million gallons (Figure 3.4). Biodiesel contains little in the way of nitrogen or sulfur compounds, so it is less polluting than conventional diesel fuel. Biodiesel is also a renewable resource because it is produced from corn, soybean,

Gasohol: Fuel Salvation or Snake Oil?

Petroleum fuels (natural gas, gasoline, diesel fuel) are the single most important materials driving the world's economy. North America has led the pack in consumption of petroleum fuels but increasing demands are being made on petroleum supplies as the populations of North America and Europe increase and the economies of China and the Indian subcontinent continue to modernize and grow. Alternative supplies of energy are being sought because the extraction, refining, and burning of oil is directly responsible for much of the pollution we experience in the developed world. In addition, it is widely anticipated that oil and natural gas supplies will run out during the twenty-first century.

One attractive alternative is ethyl alcohol (ethanol), also known as gasohol when used as a fuel. Gasohol was pioneered in Brazil, where the ethanol is produced from cane sugar. The sugary juices are expressed from the cane, fermented, and the resulting ethanol is collected by distillation. This is a highly economical process in Brazil, which has a warm climate and large land area that can be devoted to growing sugar cane. Moreover, the debris that remains after the sugary juices are expressed, called bagasse, can be used as a fuel to supply steam for the distillation and to generate electricity.

The situation is not so simple in North America, where the favored candidates for conversion to ethanol are starch and cellulose. Both require

(continued on page 44)

(continued from page 43)

enzymatic breakdown to release the sugars for fermentation, which requires additional energy, and, unlike sugar cane, the residues from corn and wheat straw have negligible fuel value. Additional energy is required to distill the ethanol. For the immediate future, most of the energy required to produce ethanol will likely come, either directly or indirectly, from crude oil and natural gas or coal-fired generating stations.

However, the hydrocarbons in gasoline contain no oxygen, but ethanol does. Because ethanol is already partially oxidized, it produces 15% to 25% less energy than an equivalent volume of gasoline. This means that a vehicle gets lower mileage with ethanol in the tank than with gasoline. There is concern in some quarters that the energy cost of ethanol production coupled with its lower energy content may mean that there is little or no real energy gain.

A partial solution to the problem of fossil fuel dependency, however, may be in the wings. A current project eyes sweet potatoes as the carbon source for ethanol production. Sweet potatoes are rich in both starch and sugars. This project proposes two parallel fermentations, anaerobic and aerobic. The first fermentation would be anaerobic and would produce methane gas (biogas). The methane would then be used as the fuel for the aerobic fermentation and distillation process that separates the ethanol. It would be effectively independent of fossil fuels and, if successful, could provide the model for future fuel-ethanol production in North America.

and other oilseed crops such as sunflower and canola. Many environmentally conscious celebrities, such as singers Neil Young and Willie Nelson, are encouraging the use of biodiesel by running their tour buses on the fuel.

In these days of concern over diminishing oil supplies, this may sound too good to be true. Could there be a downside to widespread use of biodiesel fuel? How much land do you think would have to be devoted to crops just to supply the fuel needs of the United States alone? Let's do a simple calculation,

Figure 3.4 An entrepreneur stands by the truck he uses to collect vegetable oil from restaurants to make biodiesel fuel. Biodiesel has become increasingly popular with energy-conscious people over the past few years.

using soybeans as an example. Soybeans are about 20% oil and a bushel of soybeans will yield about 1.5 gallons of biodiesel fuel. In 2005, 72 million acres of soybeans were planted in the United States, with a yield of about 3 billion bushels. At 1.5 gallons per bushel, the entire soybean crop could provide about 4.5 billion gallons of biodiesel fuel. That may sound like a lot of diesel fuel, but in 2005 farm and highway vehicles alone consumed approximately 40 billion gallons of diesel fuel. At best, then, the entire soybean crop could supply a little more than 10% of the diesel fuel required for farm and highway vehicles. And that does not take into account the fuel and fertilizer inputs, both obtained from fossil fuels, that are required to produce the soybean crop.

One solution, of course, would be to grow more soybeans, but virtually all of the arable land in North America is already under cultivation, primarily in corn, soybeans, and wheat, to provide food and raw materials used in manufacturing. The diversion of soybean and other oilseed crops away from their traditional markets would also drive up the price of food and other products. Another solution might be to identify high-oil crops that can be grown in marginal lands that are not suitable for conventional crops, but it is still unlikely that biodiesel could make more than a small dent in our consumption of petrochemical-based fuels.

Would You Like Fries or Biodiesel with Your Order?

Processing plant fats and oils to produce biodiesel is easy and relatively inexpensive, although it does require some corrosive chemicals that must be handled very carefully. In fact, biodiesel is probably the only vehicle fuel that can actually be produced at home or on the farm, and many people do just that. They start by collecting used cooking oils from their local fast-food restaurant. The fatty acids are separated from the glycerol by stirring the cooking oils with a methyl alcohol–lye mixture. After standing for a while, the mixture separates into two distinct layers, with the biodiesel (or methylated fatty acids) on top and glycerin on the bottom. An added benefit is that once the biodiesel has been siphoned off, the glycerol can be saved for use as soap or a cleaning agent. This is a great way to recycle used cooking oils, although your vehicle will smell faintly of french fries!

Summary
The role of plants in biotechnology was established long before genetic modification brought plant biotechnology to the attention of the general public. Accumulator species of plants are used to remove heavy metals from contaminated soil, a process called phytoremediation. Various forms of plant tissue culture have been used extensively to clone commercially valuable plant varieties and to eliminate viruses and other pathogens.

Plants have also been used to generate environmentally sound biofuels. Fuel ethanol is produced by fermentation of cane sugar, corn, sweet potatoes, and other plants. Biogas, or methane, is generated by the bacterial breakdown of agricultural wastes for use as an on-farm energy supply, and plant fats and oils are processed as biodiesel, a renewable fuel for buses, trucks, and automobiles.

The advantage of biofuels over fossil fuels is that the plants or plant oils used in the production of biofuels are a renewable resource, but the diversion of large amounts of crops into biofuels of any kind will compete with traditional markets and drive up the price of food and other products.

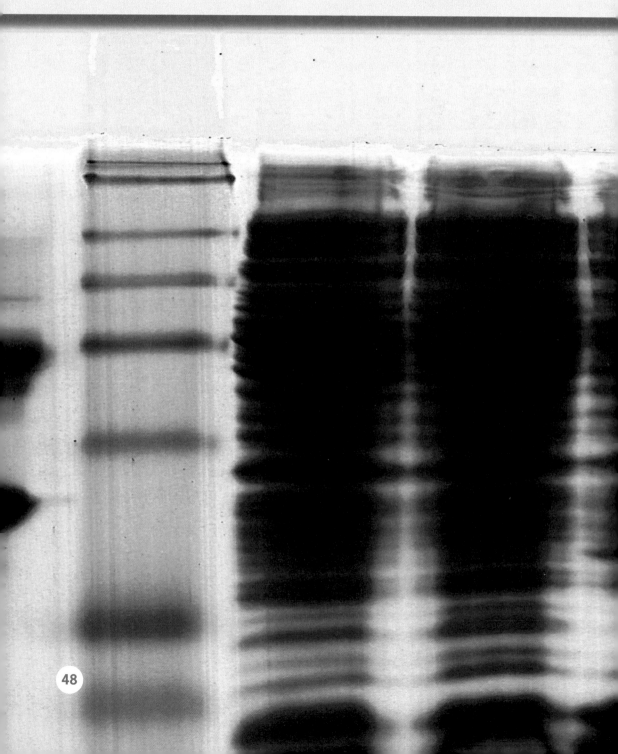

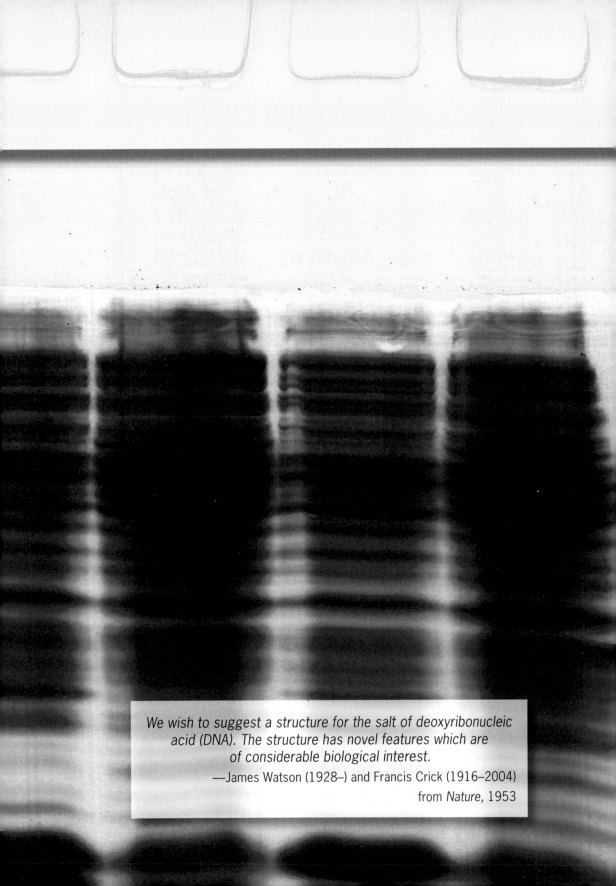

We wish to suggest a structure for the salt of deoxyribonucleic acid (DNA). The structure has novel features which are of considerable biological interest.

—James Watson (1928–) and Francis Crick (1916–2004)

from *Nature*, 1953

DNA, Genes, and Protein

Biotechnology, in the sense that most people understand it today, involves a manipulation of genes, thus "tricking" plants into producing novel proteins. This is a controversial technology for a variety of reasons, but we cannot make informed judgments about the technology and its application without at least a rudimentary understanding of the science behind it. Both the nature of the gene and the synthesis of proteins are intimately related to the hereditary DNA. Thus, in order to understand how this new technology works, we should first have a basic understanding of DNA and of the relationship between DNA and proteins.

A DNA PRIMER

Deoxyribonucleic acid (DNA) was first isolated from the nuclei of cells in 1869, but it was not until early in the twentieth century that it became clear DNA was the hereditary material that passed unique characteristics from one generation to the next. Chemical analyses eventually revealed that nucleic acids—DNA and its companion ribonucleic acid (RNA)—were very large molecules constructed from only five simple building blocks called **nucleotides**. A nucleotide is composed of three elements: a nitrogen-containing **base**, a 5-carbon (pentose) sugar, and a phosphate group (Figure 4.1). The sugar in RNA is called ribose, hence *ribo*nucleic acid. The sugar in DNA is missing one oxygen atom and is thus called *deoxy*ribose. The four bases that make up DNA are adenine, guanine, cytosine, and thymine, while in RNA uracil takes the place of thymine. Biologists had long known that heredity was controlled by genes and that genes were in some way related to DNA. Scientists knew that it was important to understand the structure of DNA because knowing the structure would lead to further understanding of how the hereditary material worked in the cell.

   The first clue to the structure of DNA came in the 1940s when Erwin Chargaff analyzed DNA from several different species and found that, regardless of the source, the DNA always contained roughly equal proportions of adenine and thymine and that the

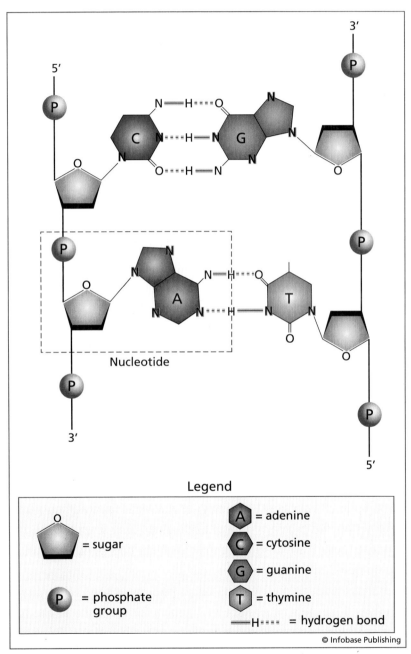

Legend

Figure 4.1 DNA is made out of a basic unit called a nucleotide. Each nucleotide is made out of a sugar molecule, a phosphate group, and a base.

proportions of cytosine and guanine were also similar. The puzzle was finally solved in 1953 by James Watson and Francis Crick, who published their results in a remarkably brief letter to the scientific journal *Nature* entitled "The Molecular Structure of Nucleic Acids: A Structure for Deoxyribose Nucleic Acid." In this letter, Watson and Crick noted that their "structure has novel features which are of considerable biological interest." Given the impact that their discovery has had on biology, agriculture, and medicine over the past 50 years, this may go down as one of the greatest understatements in the history of science.

The Watson and Crick model for DNA is often described as a ladder, twisted about its long axis to form a helix. Because there are two paired DNA molecules, it is called a double helix. The sides of the ladder are formed from alternating sugar molecules and phosphate groups. This is referred to as the sugar-phosphate

The Double Helix

The famous paper describing the structure of DNA by James Watson and Francis Crick was published in the April 25, 1953, issue of the prestigious British science journal *Nature*. At the time, Watson was a postdoctoral fellow (a recent Ph.D.) from Harvard University working with Crick at the Cavendish Laboratories in Cambridge, England. Discovering the structure of DNA was considered to be a "holy grail" of biology and several laboratories were known to be working on the problem. It was understood that knowing the structure of DNA would more than likely reveal to scientists how DNA was able to store and pass on hereditary information.

One of those working on DNA was Linus Pauling at the California Institute of Technology. Pauling was already well known for his work on the nature of the chemical bond and would go on to be awarded the Nobel Prize in Chemistry in 1954 for his earlier work on the structure of another complicated "backbone." The rungs of the ladder—and the key to the Watson and Crick hypothesis—are the paired bases: adenine (A) is always paired with thymine (T) and guanine (G) is always paired with cytosine (C). The bases pair up in these combinations because of the way they bond to each other. The opposing nucleotides are held together by weak **hydrogen bonds**; cytosine and guanine are held together by three hydrogen bonds but only two bonds are formed between adenine and thymine. In addition to the bonding, the shape and the space occupied by the four molecules means this is the only way they can fit together without distorting the sugar-phosphate backbone. The consistent pairing of A with T and G with C also explains Chargaff's earlier data.

There is a second important consequence of the pairing of A with T and G with C that is fundamental to the way DNA works. The two halves, or strands, of the DNA molecule are

macromolecule, protein. However, Watson and Crick won the DNA race primarily because they had access to one critical piece of evidence: an X-ray diffraction pattern of DNA provided by Rosalind Franklin and Maurice Wilkins of the University College of London. When an X-ray beam is fired at a crystal structure, the beam is scattered (or diffracted) in a particular pattern, depending on the arrangement of molecules in the crystal lattice. The diffraction pattern obtained by Franklin and Wilkins indicated that their DNA crystals were arranged in a helical pattern.

Watson and Crick put this information together with what was then known about the chemistry of DNA—in particular, the very consistent ratios of adenine (A) plus thymine (T) and cytosine (C) plus guanine (G)—and began to build models as big as themselves from pieces of wire and bits of brass. The one model in which everything finally "fit together" was the now-famous double helix.

complementary. Wherever one strand has an A, the complementary strand will have a T. Where the strand has a G, the complementary strand will have a C, and so forth. Each strand of nucleotides also has polarity and the two strands are **antiparallel.** Antiparallel means that when the two strands are paired, their polarity is reversed. If one strand can be said to run north to south, the complementary strand runs south to north.

Complementarity provides the key to how DNA is able to replicate itself so precisely during cell division. The hydrogen bonds that hold complementary base pairs together are relatively weak chemical bonds, so the two strands can easily be separated. When DNA replicates itself, an enzyme called **helicase** simply splits the molecule down the middle, separating the two strands of paired nucleotides (Figure 4.2). Once the two strands are separated, the base sequence in each strand then serves as a template (pattern) to reconstruct its complementary strand. Free nucleotides pair up with their complement on the single strand and an enzyme called **DNA ligase** connects the adjacent sugar and phosphate groups to form the new backbone. The result is two exact copies of the original double-stranded DNA.

WHAT IS A GENE?

DNA is a lot like the hard drive on your computer—its primary function is to store information. Like the information in your hard drive, the information in DNA is stored in discrete blocks or addresses. These blocks or addresses are called **genes.** In a computer, the information needed to perform specific operations is downloaded into the RAM, which is where the instructions in the software are actually carried out. In the cell, the information contained in the gene (the DNA) is downloaded into ribonucleic acid (RNA) which, in turn, directs the synthesis of the proteins that make the cell function.

To put it in biochemical terms, DNA is a sequence of nucleotides and a protein molecule is a sequence of amino acids. *A gene is a*

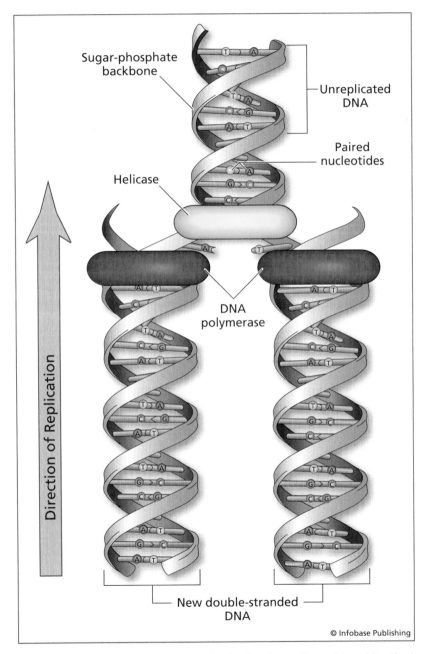

Figure 4.2 DNA replication results in the formation of two identical double-stranded DNA molecules. Enzymes, such as helicase and DNA polymerase, are essential to the process.

particular sequence of nucleotides within the DNA that specifies the sequence of amino acids in a particular protein. By controlling which proteins are produced by an individual cell, the gene controls the characteristics of that cell and, consequently, the characteristics of tissues, organs, and organisms. Proteins, and consequently genes, vary in length, but most genes are approximately 1,000 to 4,000 nucleotides long. The entire complement of genes in an organism's DNA is called the **genome**.

PROTEINS AND THE GENETIC CODE

There are more proteins in a cell than any other single organic molecule, and they perform a vast variety of functions. The biggest single class of proteins is the enzymes, proteins that catalyze biochemical reactions (including the synthesis of other proteins). A typical cell may contain as many as 3,000 enzymes. Other proteins carry messages between cells or contribute to the structure of membranes and other cell components.

Proteins are long chains of amino acids. There are 20 standard amino acids that can be assembled in a nearly infinite number of combinations to produce this large array of proteins. The amino acid sequence determines the structure of the protein and the structure determines its function in the cell. In most proteins, the amino acid chain twists, coils, and folds back on itself to form an intricately shaped molecule. The shape of a protein is very sensitive to the amino acid composition, and a change of a single amino acid can have a profound effect on the ability of a protein to assume its proper shape and carry out its function.

One example is herbicide resistance in plants. There is a family of herbicides—the triazines—that kills plants by interfering with photosynthesis. It does this by binding to a small protein in the chloroplast. The change of one amino acid in that protein changes the protein just enough so that the herbicide can no longer bind, but the change does not impair the normal photosynthetic function of the protein. So, it takes only a single amino acid change in one small protein to confer triazine resistance on the plant. Triazine-resistance is a common occurrence in weeds because this kind of subtle mutation occurs often in nature.

As noted above, DNA is not directly involved in protein synthesis. Instead, the DNA is unzipped and the information in the gene is **transcribed** into messenger RNA (mRNA). That is, rather than making a complementary DNA strand as in DNA replication, the DNA template is used to make a complementary strand of RNA. Messenger RNA is identical to a single strand of DNA except that it contains a ribose sugar and thymine is replaced by uracil. The RNA, which now contains a copy of the genetic code, then moves out of the nucleus into the cytoplasm, where it binds to a protein aggregate called the ribosome. The mRNA-ribosome complex is now ready to carry out the DNA's instructions and direct the synthesis, or **translation**, of protein (Figure 4.3).

How can a code using only four "letters"—the four different bases in a DNA molecule—specify the assembly of at least 20 different amino acids into literally thousands of different proteins? DNA actually uses a three-letter, or triplet, code based on a sequence of three nucleotides. Each triplet, or **codon**, is the code that specifies one amino acid. The number of possible combinations for combining 4 bases into groups of 3 is 4 cubed (4^3), or 64, so there are at least three times as many codons as are necessary to encode only 20 amino acids. In fact, most amino acids are encoded by multiple codons. In addition, there is also one codon that signals the starting point for protein translation and three stop codons that signal the end of translation.

The genetic code is universal: the same code is used by bacteria, plants, fruit flies, and humans. This means that the gene encoding human insulin, for example, can be inserted into a bacterium and the bacterium will transcribe the gene and translate it into insulin the same way that human pancreatic cells do.

There is, however, a bit more to a gene than just the amino acid sequence of a protein. For example, the DNA sequence that

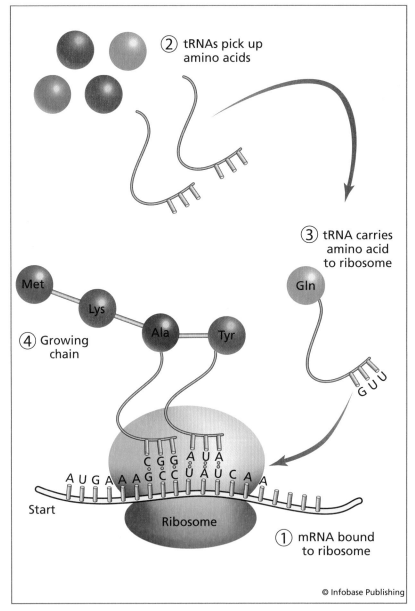

Figure 4.3 During translation, transfer RNA (tRNA) carry amino acids to the cell's ribosomes. Each tRNA molecule recognizes a sequence of three nucleotides, known as a codon, on a strand of messenger RNA (mRNA). A protein is created when the amino acids are chained together.

codes for human insulin is over 4,000 bases long. With a code of three bases for one amino acid, there is enough DNA to code for over 1,300 amino acids, but insulin is a small protein that contains just over 100 amino acids. What is the purpose of that extra DNA?

The Genetic Code

Each amino acid in a protein is specified by a sequence of three nucleotides in the DNA of the gene. When cellular conditions call for the synthesis of a particular protein, one strand of the DNA is transcribed into messenger RNA (mRNA). Messenger RNA is a single-stranded nucleic acid that carries the message of the gene into the cytoplasm, where the protein is actually synthesized. So, the three-letter codes (codons) for the various amino acids are expressed in terms of the sequence of nucleotides in the mRNA rather than DNA. This distinction is important because (a) the nucleotide composition of RNA is complementary to the coding strand of DNA and (b) where the DNA contains an adenine molecule, the complementary strand of RNA will incorporate uracil rather than thymine. As a result, the codons in the mRNA will include U in place of T.

A simplified version of how the code directs protein synthesis is illustrated in Figure 4.3. First, mRNA binds to a cytoplasmic protein unit called the ribosome. Then, transfer RNA (tRNA) binds to a specific amino acid and carries (or transfers) it to the mRNA. Each molecule of tRNA includes a sequence of nucleotides called an anti-codon, which is complementary to the codon for the amino acid that it carries. The anti-codon binds to the codon on the mRNA, lining up the tRNA in the proper position so that its amino acid can be added to the growing amino acid chain. Each time a new amino acid is added to the chain, the ribosome shifts one codon, or three nucleotides, downstream on the mRNA, preparing it to receive the tRNA for the next amino acid in the sequence.

As shown in the illustration, the codon for the amino acid alanine (Ala) is GCC, so the anti-codon on the tRNA is complementary, or CGG. Similarly, for tyrosine (Tyr) the codon is UAU, so the anti-codon is AUA. The start codon, AUG, is also the codon for the amino acid methionine, so all proteins begin with a methionine unit.

It turns out that a gene is more like a recipe—it contains not only the list of ingredients (the amino acids), but also the instructions for making the protein. Sectors of the gene (promoters, introns, etc.) contain the instructions that tell the cell when to make the protein, how much to make, and so on.

THE BIRTH OF MODERN BIOTECHNOLOGY

Bacteria have to contend with viruses just as humans do. Bacterial viruses, called **bacteriophages** or simply phages, are little more than a piece of DNA surrounded by a coat of protein. The phage infects the bacterium by attaching to the surface of the host cell and injecting its DNA into the cell. Once inside, the viral DNA takes over the synthetic machinery of the bacterium and directs the unlucky host to replicate more viral DNA and protein. Eventually, the host cell ruptures and the new generation of viruses is released into the environment.

It is difficult to say exactly when genetic engineering began, but certainly the discovery of **restriction enzymes** was an important first step. Some bacteria are protected from phages because they contain enzymes that can cut foreign DNA into shorter pieces that are unable to replicate. Because these enzymes *restrict* viral

Restricting Restriction Enzymes

You may wonder why a bacterium that produces restriction enzymes doesn't digest its own DNA. It is because some of the bacterial DNA nucleotides have been methylated. The addition of a few strategically placed methyl groups ($-CH_3$) at the restriction site prevents the restriction enzymes from digesting the bacterial DNA. Of course, nature is a constant battle with one group trying to get ahead of the other, so it is not too surprising that some phages have evolved methylation as a way of gaining an edge over the bacterium and avoiding being attacked by restriction enzymes in the host cell.

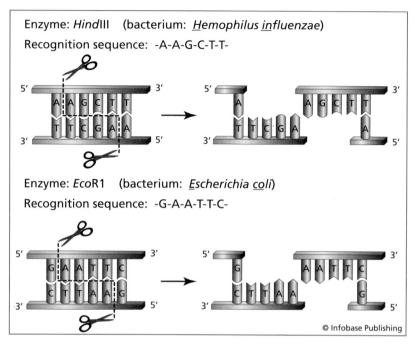

Figure 4.4 Restriction enzymes, such as *Hind*III and *Eco*R1, act as biological scissors. They allow scientists to cut DNA and recombine it into new configurations.

replication, they were called restriction enzymes. The first restriction enzyme (called *Hind*III) to be discovered was isolated and characterized by Hamilton Smith, a researcher at Johns Hopkins University in 1970. In 1978, Smith shared the Nobel Prize with two others for their discoveries of restriction enzymes.

There are now hundreds of restriction enzymes available from a diverse array of bacteria. Each one cuts DNA at a unique point identified by a particular sequence of base pairs. The enzyme *Eco*R1, for example, recognizes the sequence GAATTC and cuts the DNA between G and A, while *Hind*III recognizes the sequence AAGCTT and cuts between the two A's (Figure 4.4). *Eco*R1 has a preeminent place in the history of bioengineering. In the early 1970s, Paul Berg at Stanford University isolated DNA from two sources: the bacterium *Escherichia coli* and a primate virus called SV40. He cut both samples of DNA with *EcoR*1 and then mixed the two in a test tube. The result was a hybrid molecule of SV40 and *E. coli* DNA. Because the new DNA was created by splicing together (or recombining) DNA from two different sources, it was called **recombinant DNA** (rDNA). With this experiment, Berg created the first recombinant DNA molecule, thus making genetic modification possible and providing the foundation for all of modern biotechnology. Berg's work was recognized with the Nobel Prize in 1980.

At the same time, Stanley Cohen and Herbert Boyer, also at Stanford, were studying bacterial **plasmids**. Plasmids are interesting little pieces of DNA that are found primarily in bacteria. Plasmids are very small, circular pieces of DNA that are separate from the normal chromosomal DNA of the bacterium. One of the principal functions of plasmids appears to be to carry genes that confer resistance to antibiotics. Cohen and Boyer found that if they cut plasmids from two different sources with the enzyme *EcoR*1, the two plasmids would readily join to form a hybrid plasmid. This is because when *EcoR*1 cuts the DNA, it leaves overhanging, or "sticky" ends. They are called "sticky" ends because when any two pieces of DNA cut by this enzyme are brought together, they naturally anneal, or "stick" together. The same thing will happen with a piece of "foreign" DNA—say from the chromosome of another organism—that has been cut out with the same enzyme. All pieces of DNA cut by *EcoR*1 will anneal with a similarly treated plasmid to form a hybrid plasmid (Figure 4.5).

Cohen and Boyer then took advantage of another peculiar trait of bacteria—their capacity to take up bits of DNA from their environment and incorporate it into their own genome. This process is called **transformation,** and the bacterium that takes up the foreign DNA is said to be transformed. Cohen and Boyer found they could induce bacteria to take up hybrid plasmid DNA. Once inside the cell, the plasmid (including any newly introduced genes) is replicated normally as the bacteria divide. Under optimal laboratory conditions, *E. coli* may divide every 20 to 30 minutes, so that after

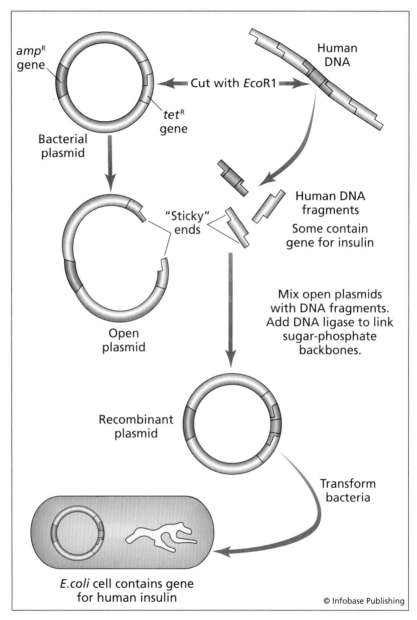

Figure 4.5 Restriction enzymes are used to create recombinant, or hybrid, plasmids. In the illustration above, the restriction enzyme *Eco*R1 is used to insert the gene for insulin into a bacterial plasmid. The recombinant plasmid is incorporated into an *E. coli* cell by a process known as transformation.

8 hours of laboratory culture, a single *E. coli* will give rise to over 16 million progeny. Each cell contains an exact copy of the plasmid with the newly introduced gene. This replication of the genes to produce zillions of exact copies is called gene cloning. (No, zillions is not an official numerical unit, but it is an easy way to express a really big number.)

Transformation is not 100% efficient, so there has to be some method for selecting the cells that were successfully transformed and contain the desired DNA. For this, Cohen and Boyer developed another little trick. They used a plasmid that contained *two* different antibiotic resistance genes: one gene for ampicillin resistance (*amp R*) and one for tetracycline resistance (*tet R*). The DNA fragment containing the gene to be cloned was then inserted at a restriction site within the *tet R* gene. This disrupts that gene and prevents the synthesis of the resistance protein. Genes such as *amp R* and *tet R* are called **marker genes** because they identify, or mark, the cells that have been successfully transformed.

Using a technique called replica plating, the culture is "plated out" on a medium that contains ampicillin. This technique spreads a dilute bacterial culture on the surface of an agar medium in a petri dish. After a period of incubation, each live bacterium will give rise to a small, visible colony of cells but, because the medium contains ampicillin, only transformed cells having the ampicillin resistance gene will produce colonies. A sterile pad is then pressed against the colonies on the ampicillin plate. Some of the cells from each colony will be picked up by the pad, which is then pressed on the surface of a second plate containing tetracycline. This transfers a few cells from each colony to the tetracycline medium *in the exact image* of the ampicillin plate. Cells that contain the recombinant plasmid will form colonies on the ampicillin plate but will not grow and form colonies on the tetracycline plate. It is then easy enough to identify which colonies grew on ampicillin but not on tetracycline—those are the colonies that have been transformed with the recombinant DNA.

With these experiments, the stage was now set. We have:

- **Restriction enzymes** that allow scientists to cut DNA in specific locations and insert new DNA to make recombinant DNA (rDNA). The new DNA inserted could be a specific sequence of nucleotides, that is, a gene.

- **Plasmids** that, through the process of bacterial transformation, provide a vehicle, or **vector,** for inserting the new DNA into another organism.

- **Marker genes** that enable the scientists to screen a culture and select for the cells that have been transformed with the rDNA.

These experiments heralded the arrival of an entirely new way to modify cells.

DNA Fingerprinting: An Organism's Bar Code

DNA fingerprinting is one of the latest technologies to help forensic investigators bring the truth to light. In the world of criminal investigation, DNA fingerprinting has helped to convict guilty parties and has led to the release of falsely convicted individuals. Just what is this new technology?

DNA fingerprinting is a way of looking at the unique signature found in an individual's genetic makeup, and it is made possible by the use of restriction enzymes. First, the investigator needs to obtain a sample of DNA. A milliliter of fresh whole blood is an ideal sample, but the polymerase chain reaction (PCR) can be used to amplify the quantity of DNA if the original sample is very small (for example, saliva on an envelope, a hair follicle, or a blood stain). Detergents are used to extract and purify the DNA or it can be mechanically forced out of the cell through a syringe. The purified DNA is then cut with restriction enzymes.

(continued on page 66)

(continued from page 65)

After the restriction enzymes have done their job, the mixture of DNA fragments of various sizes must be separated. This is done using a technique known as electrophoresis. The sample containing the DNA fragments is applied in a narrow well at one end of thin layer of a gelatinous medium and an electrical current is applied. The DNA fragments are negatively charged, so they move through the gel toward the positively charged electrode. The fragments are sorted according to size as they move through the gel because their movement is restricted by pores in the gel. Smaller fragments are less restricted by the pores and so will travel further through the gel than the larger fragments.

The next step is to visualize the position of the different fragments on the gel. This is done by first heating the gel to split the double-stranded DNA into single strands and then transferring the strands to a nitrocellulose membrane. The fragments are permanently fixed to the surface of the membrane where they can be located with a probe. A probe is a small, single-stranded fragment of DNA that has been made radioactive and that contains the complementary code for a specific sequence of bases. The probe will bind with the DNA on the membrane wherever the complementary base sequence is found.

Finally, a sheet of X-ray film is placed against the membrane. Because the probes are radioactive they emit energy that exposes the film. When the film is developed, the positions of the various DNA fragments are indicated by a series of black lines that vary by position and intensity (amount), just like the bar codes on manufactured products. The "bar code" is the DNA fingerprint. The image on the X-ray film may include 40 or more bands, and because different samples are run side by side on the same gel, they may be compared directly. The odds that DNA restriction fragments from two people will match all 40 bands, unless they are identical twins, are extremely low.

DNA fingerprinting is not limited to forensic situations or humans. DNA fingerprinting can be used to establish the relatedness of virtually any organism, including plants.

Summary

DNA is a relatively uncomplicated, double-stranded molecule, consisting of only four building blocks called deoxyribonucleotides. The key to DNA structure is that opposing nucleotides in the two strands pair in a complementary relationship: the adenine nucleotide (A) pairs only with the thymine nucleotide (T) and the guanine nucleotide (G) pairs only with the cytosine nucleotide (C). The geometry of these pairings is responsible for maintaining the parallel spacing of the sugar-phosphate backbone of the molecule as it twists to form a helix.

The complementarity of nucleotide pairing is also the key to both DNA replication and RNA synthesis. As the two strands separate, free nucleotides naturally pair with each single strand to form a new double-stranded molecule. In the same way, ribonucleotides pair with complementary bases in the DNA template to form a strand of messenger RNA that moves into the cytoplasm of the cell where it directs protein synthesis. The DNA code is based on the sequence of nucleotides, with each sequence of three nucleotides coding for a specific amino acid in the protein. The entire sequence of DNA nucleotides that specifies a complete protein is known as a gene.

Limited sequences of DNA, some containing a complete gene, can be isolated by cutting the DNA with restriction enzymes. Pieces of DNA can then be recombined in different combinations to form recombinant DNA (rDNA). Bacteria have the capacity to take up pieces of DNA from their environment and incorporate it into their own genome. A bacterium that has incorporated a foreign gene is said to have been transformed. As the transformed bacterium reproduces, it produces many copies of that gene, a process called gene cloning.

5 Engineering Plants

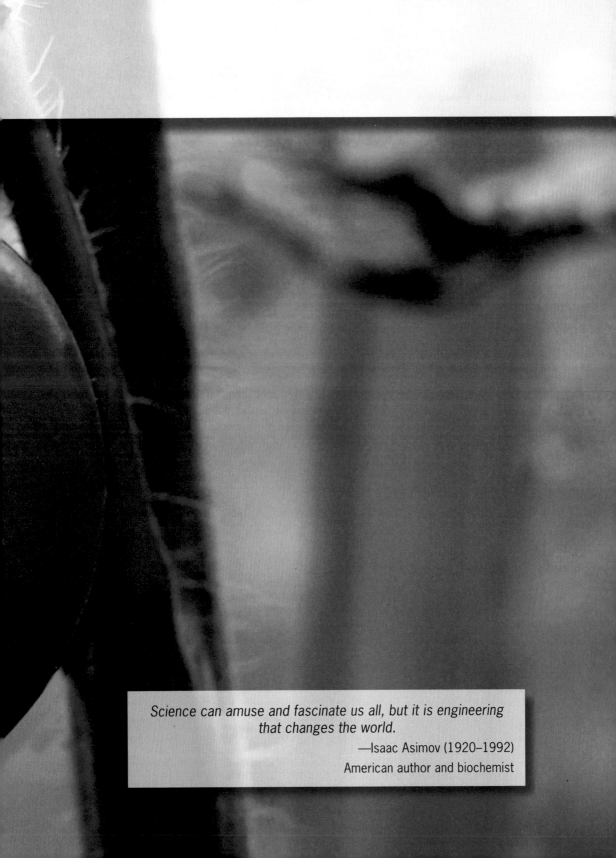

Science can amuse and fascinate us all, but it is engineering that changes the world.

—Isaac Asimov (1920–1992)
American author and biochemist

Engineering Plants

A noted cookbook writer of the Victorian era began her recipe for jugged hare (rabbit stew) with the instructions: "First, catch your hare." The recipe for genetic engineering is not a lot different. Before you can start moving genes around in order to create a **transgenic** plant, you have to first identify and isolate the gene of interest. Random DNA fragments are of little value if you don't know which fragment contains the gene you want to transfer. It would be like looking for that needle in the haystack. In fact, if the restriction enzymes you used to break up the DNA happened to cut the DNA in the middle of the gene you want, then no fragments will contain an intact copy of the gene.

So, we are now faced with two questions. How do we find and clone a gene that we want to use to transform a plant? And once we have the gene, how do we insert that gene into a plant? In other words, how do we actually go about genetically engineering a plant?

GENE HUNTERS

One approach to finding a particular gene is to create a complementary DNA (cDNA) library; cDNA is made by running RNA transcription in reverse. First, you have to isolate the messenger RNA (mRNA) from cells that contain the gene you are interested in. Then, an enzyme called **reverse transcriptase** is mixed with this isolated mRNA. Reverse transcriptase uses the mRNA as a template to make a single strand of DNA in the same way that DNA serves as a template for making the mRNA. Remember that making a copy of mRNA from DNA is called transcription, so making a copy of DNA from RNA is going the other way; that is, *reverse* transcription.

The enzyme reverse transcriptase is isolated from retroviruses. Most animal viruses contain DNA as their genetic material. When a virus invades a cell, it takes over the cell's genetic machinery in order to make copies of its own DNA. But there are some viruses, called retroviruses, that contain RNA instead of DNA. When a retrovirus invades a host cell, it uses a portion of its RNA to direct the synthesis of the enzyme reverse transcriptase. The reverse transcriptase then catalyzes the reverse transcription of DNA, using the viral RNA as a template. Once the DNA has been synthesized, it is then replicated using the host cell machinery. The viral DNA then instructs the host cell to produce the other bits and pieces necessary for virus multiplication. The human immunodeficiency virus (HIV) is a familiar example of an animal retrovirus. Most plant viruses are also RNA viruses (Figure 5.1).

After the cDNA strand has been synthesized, it must be cloned and the bacterial colonies grown as described in the previous chapter. The individual colonies are then stored, usually in a freezer, and this is the cDNA library. Unfortunately, there is no card catalog for this library, so you must test each colony until you find those that contain the gene you want.

There is, however, a unique advantage to using cDNA for building this library. Because cDNA is made from mRNA, it ignores inactive genes and represents only genes that were actively being expressed in the cell at the time the mRNA was isolated. This means that if you know that the protein you are interested in was being synthesized at the time (and you have selected the right restriction enzyme or enzymes), there is a much better chance that the gene of interest will be located on one of the cDNA strands.

Another method for obtaining a gene is called **reverse engineering**. If you don't know anything about the sequence of a particular gene, you can often work back from the protein that it encodes. Most proteins are easily isolated and purified, and the method for determining the amino acid sequence of a protein is now a pretty routine laboratory exercise. Once you know the amino acid sequence, it is relatively easy to synthesize a DNA strand that encodes for those amino acids in that sequence.

A third technique for coming up with new genes is to alter the DNA by inducing mutations. A mutation is nothing more than

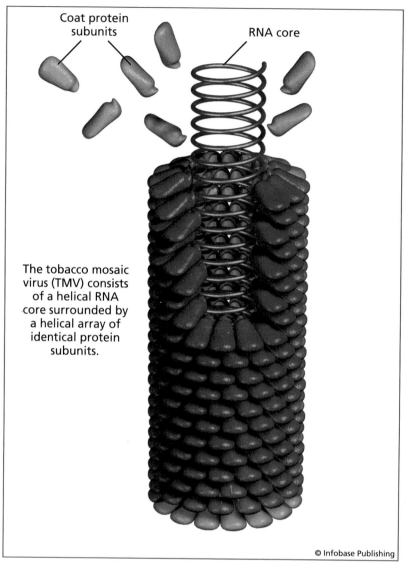

Coat protein
subunits

RNA core

The tobacco mosaic
virus (TMV) consists
of a helical RNA
core surrounded by
a helical array of
identical protein
subunits.

© Infobase Publishing

Figure 5.1 The tobacco mosaic virus (TMV) infects the leaves, flowers, and fruit of many plants, including tobacco. TMV is an extremely persistent plant virus and has been known to survive for many years in dried plant parts.

a change—any change—in the DNA of an organism. Mutations occur naturally with a much greater frequency than you might imagine, although the truth is that most mutations are not terribly beneficial. Occasionally, however, a mutation appears that gives the organism an edge and evolution takes a tiny step forward.

It is not difficult to induce mutations in plants. Mutations can easily be induced by exposing seeds or very young seedlings to **ionizing radiation** or **chemical mutagens**. One popular chemical mutagen is ethyl methane sulfonate (EMS)—a very nasty and highly toxic chemical. Of course, if the level of radiation or EMS dose is too high, the seedlings will probably die from radiation or chemical poisoning. At lower doses, however, a few seedlings will survive and can be screened for a new and desirable trait.

There is one more method and that is to find another organism that has the gene you want. This is one of the most controversial aspects of genetic engineering—creating **transgenic** plants.

TRANSFORMING PLANT CELLS: PROTOPLASTS AND GENE GUNS

Once you have found the gene you are interested in and have cloned it, the next trick is to get that piece of DNA into a plant cell. Unlike bacteria, plants do not spontaneously take up bits of DNA from their environment. So how, then, does the genetic engineer transform plants?

To begin with, whole plants are not transformed. Instead, one transforms either cells in tissue culture (described in the micropropagation section in chapter 3) or **protoplasts**. Protoplasts are naked plant cells that have been treated with a mixture of enzymes, including cellulase, that strip away the cell walls and leave only the protoplasm surrounded by a cell membrane. Removing the cell wall, however, creates certain problems for plant cells, because they depend on the strength and rigidity of the cell wall to keep intact. Without the cell wall, water will continue to diffuse into the protoplast by **osmosis** and the protoplast will swell until it ruptures. In order to get around this problem, plant protoplasts must be maintained in a medium containing a high concentration of solute such as mannitol, a sugar alcohol. The high solute concentration

Polymerase Chain Reaction

It is much easier to transform a plant or other organism if you have many copies of a gene to work with. Bacteria can be used to clone or make multiple copies of genes, but now it is more common to use a method called the polymerase chain reaction (PCR). A PCR machine is sort of like a photocopier for genes.

The basis for a PCR machine is a temperature-regulated block that can both heat and cool very rapidly. The sample chamber in the block is loaded with a sample of DNA that contains the gene, some enzymes (DNA polymerase and ligase), and a supply of each of the four nucleotides that make up DNA. Also in the mix are primers, short pieces of DNA that have been constructed to bind with the DNA at either end of the gene. Primers select the target gene to be amplified and help to avoid copying the entire genome.

The reaction is started by heating the sample to about 95°C (200°F), which separates the double-stranded DNA into single strands. The sample is then cooled to about 60°C (140°F), but before the two strands can reunite, the primers get in the way by binding to the DNA. DNA polymerase then fills in the gaps between the two primers and DNA ligase "zips" the newly inserted nucleotides together to form a new DNA strand. There are now two exact copies of the original DNA. The heating-cooling cycle is repeated to produce 4 copies, then 8, then 16, and so forth. Every time the cycle is repeated, the number of copies is doubled; 20 cycles will produce approximately 2^{20} or more than 1 million copies from a single starting molecule.

Most proteins are denatured or inactivated at temperatures near 95°C (200°F), but the DNA polymerase used in PCR is a special form obtained from bacteria that are adapted to life in hot springs. You may also have wondered how forensic scientists can do DNA fingerprinting with DNA from a single hair, spot of blood, or other microscopic sample. The answer is that they use PCR to amplify the DNA.

balances the osmotic properties of the surrounding medium with the osmotic properties of the protoplast so that the protoplast does not take up excess water. Incidentally, animal cells, which do not have a cell wall, avoid this problem because they have mechanisms for pumping water out of the cell to control cell volume. Plant cells lack such pumping mechanisms.

Protoplasts can be isolated from virtually any plant tissue, although leaf cells are most commonly used. Most protoplasts are capable of continued cell division when cultured in an appropriate medium. However, once the enzymes are removed from the medium, protoplasts will quickly regenerate cell walls. The cells can then be stimulated to form embryo-like cell clusters and, eventually, shoots and roots and intact, fertile plants.

Under the right conditions, protoplasts from two different sources can be induced to fuse, forming single hybrid cells called **somatic hybrids**. The term *somatic hybrid* refers to hybrids formed by fusion of vegetative cells rather than normal reproductive cells (sperm and eggs). Somatic hybridization is an important tool for combining useful characteristics from different organisms. For example, many wild species of the genus *Solanum* have resistance to major diseases of the potato (*Solanum tuberosum*). However, genetic improvement of the potato is hindered because the wild species are sexually incompatible with the potato and cannot be crossbred with potato plants in the normal manner. Protoplast fusion is one way to circumvent pollen sterility or other incompatibility barriers and introduce new characteristics into crop species. Protoplast fusion as a way to improve crops is also being explored in citrus (oranges and grapefruits) and cereal grains (rice and wheat) and to produce new floral colors in horticultural species such as petunias.

Protoplasts are particularly useful to the bioengineer because the absence of a cell wall makes it easier to insert DNA directly into the cell. One technique is called **electroporation**. In this technique, the protoplasts are suspended in a liquid medium along with microscopic gold beads that have been coated with pieces of DNA. The protoplasts are then subjected to a brief pulse of electrical current (typically measured in milliseconds). The electrical pulse opens up small holes in the cell membrane that allow the DNA-coated beads to enter the protoplast. The membrane quickly reseals itself and the DNA remains trapped within the protoplast. Some of the DNA then becomes incorporated into the host cell's genome and is reproduced along with the rest of the DNA when the cell divides.

Another way of transforming plant cells is literally a "shotgun" approach. In this technique, known as biolistics, the DNA is first coated on gold or tungsten beads approximately 1 micrometer (0.000039 inch) in diameter. The particles are then loaded into a "**gene gun**," which fires them at a suspension of cultured cells (Figure 5.2). The gene gun was originally developed in the early 1980s by a group of plant biologists and **nanotechnologists** (technologists who work with very small things) at Cornell University. The particles, fired by a discharge of high-pressure helium gas, travel at about 400 meters per second. This is fast enough to penetrate the cell membranes and carry the DNA into the cells but not so fast that the discharge destroys the cells. Believe it or not, in the early days of the gene gun technique, some laboratories actually used modified 0.22-caliber rifles! The gene gun technique has been particularly useful for transforming corn or maize (*Zea mays*) cells, which do not lend themselves to protoplast-based techniques.

NATURE'S OWN GENETIC ENGINEER
The most widely used vector for introducing foreign genes into plants takes us back to bacteria and plasmids. A curious pathological condition that affects many species of plants is a cancerous growth that commonly appears on stems (Figure 5.3). Perhaps you have seen one in a local garden. This growth, called **crown gall**, shows us that nature discovered genetic engineering long before we did.

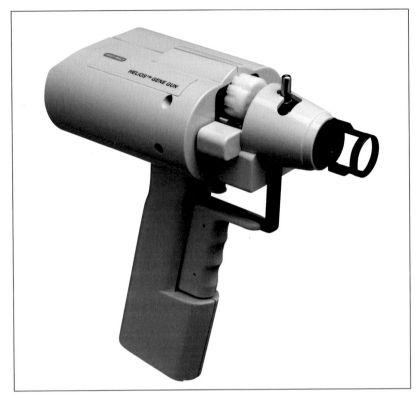

Figure 5.2 A gene gun can be used to inject foreign DNA into a plant cell. The foreign DNA is coated on metal beads and then fired at a collection of plant cells. Once inside the cell, the DNA releases from the bead and becomes incorporated into the plant chromosome.

Crown gall is caused by a common soil bacterium called *Agrobacterium tumifaciens* (we will call it *Agrobacter,* for short). The genes that enable *Agrobacter* to cause crown gall are not particularly unusual—they are genes that encode enzymes for the synthesis of two naturally occurring plant hormones called auxin and cytokinin. In the plant, auxin normally causes cells to enlarge and cytokinin normally stimulates cells to divide. The auxin and cytokinin genes are not expressed in the bacterium. However, when the bacterium invades a plant, normally at the site of a wound, it transforms the plant by integrating the hormone genes into the DNA of the infected plant cell. The transformed plant cell then

Figure 5.3 A crown gall is the result of an infection by a common soil bacterium, *Agrobacterium tumifaciens*. The unique properties of this bacterium have made it a useful tool in genetic engineering of plants.

synthesizes higher-than-normal amounts of the two hormones. Overproduction of auxin and cytokinin causes the infected cells to enlarge and divide more rapidly than normal and leads to an uncontrolled cancerous type of growth. The bacterium *Agrobacter* is thus a natural genetic engineer.

Scientists have learned to use the engineering skills of *Agrobacter* as an efficient way to introduce new genes into plants. The bacterium carries the hormone genes on a Ti (tumor-inducing) plasmid. The first step is to disarm the plasmid by removing the hormone genes. A bacterium carrying the disarmed plasmid can still invade plant cells, but without the hormone genes it is unable to cause tumors. The second step is to replace the hormone genes with a foreign gene of choice. When the bacterium carrying the engineered plasmid infects cells of the target plant, the new gene becomes incorporated into the host cell DNA and is expressed along with all of the other host cell genes.

Agrobacter is most commonly used to transform disks of tissue cut from leaves, where the bacteria infect the wound cells at the edge of the disk. Once transformation is complete, the bacteria are killed off with an antibiotic and the leaf disks can be manipulated in culture to produce shoots and roots. Unfortunately, *Agrobacter* infects only dicotyledenous plants (plants with two cotyledons or seed leaves in the seed) such as beans and peas. This means that plants with only one cotyledon (monocotyledonous plants), such as corn and wheat, are most commonly transformed by using the gene gun technique.

HERBICIDE TOLERANCE: HOW GENETIC ENGINEERING WORKS

You may have heard of the herbicide Roundup™. Plants engineered to tolerate (or resist) this herbicide have received a lot of publicity and are probably the most widely known example of **GMO**s worldwide. Plants engineered for herbicide tolerance were the first genetically engineered plants to be released for two reasons. First, herbicide tolerance usually involves only one gene, so the engineering is relatively simple. Second, as we will see in chapter 6, there appeared to be both an obvious benefit and a ready market for the product.

Roundup™ is a trade name for a chemical compound called **glyphosate,** an herbicide that kills plants by blocking the synthesis of the so-called aromatic amino acids: tryptophan, phenylalanine, and tyrosine (Figure 5.4). Without those amino acids, the plant is unable to synthesize proteins and it dies of protein starvation. Glyphosate acts by inhibiting the activity of an enzyme, enolpyr-uvyl-shikimate-3-phosphate synthase (EPSPS), that catalyzes a critical step in the synthesis of those three amino acids. Scientists looked at EPSPS in a variety of species and found a variant in petunia cells that was several times less sensitive to glyphosate inhibition than the normal enzyme. Using rDNA technology, they coupled this enzyme to a particularly active promoter (the piece of DNA that activates or turns on the gene). Plants that are transformed with this new combination of gene and promoter will **overexpress** the gene for the more tolerant enzyme. The term *overexpression* means that the cells produce higher-than-normal amounts of the messenger RNA for the resistant enzyme. Cells with more of the resistant enzyme will naturally tolerate higher doses of the enzyme inhibitor.

Another example is the herbicide **glufosinate,** marketed under the trademark Liberty™. Glufosinate also inhibits an enzyme, but this enzyme is involved in a complex set of reactions that incorpo-rates nitrogen into amino acids. Plants take up nitrogen from the soil in the form of nitrate (NO^{3-}) and convert it to ammonium ion (NH^{4+}) which, under normal circumstances, is incorporated immediately into amino acids. Glufosinate blocks this last step, leaving the ammonium ion to accumulate in the cells. Unfor-tunately, free ammonium ion is highly toxic and it doesn't take too much to kill the cells. Here, a fungus comes to the rescue: *Streptomyces hygroscopicus* is a common soil fungus that secretes a chemical inhibitor, or fungicide, called bialaphos. But how do

Figure 5.4 Two test plots of soybeans are pictured side by side. The soybeans treated with Roundup™ herbicide (*right*) show less weed growth than the soybeans that have not been treated with Roundup™ (*left*).

organisms protect themselves against toxic substances that they themselves secrete? *S. hygroscopicus* resolves this problem by also producing an enzyme that deactivates bialaphos. Fortunately, at least for genetic engineers, this enzyme also deactivates other chemicals, such as glufosinate, that have a chemical structure similar to bialaphos. This means that plants engineered with the fungal gene for the enzyme may continue to take up glufosinate but will deactivate the herbicide before it can do any damage to the plant.

The question of human toxicity naturally arises when discussing pesticides in general and extensive use of herbicides such as glyphosate and glufosinate in particular. Glyphosate and glufosinate are not generally toxic to animals and humans because they target specific enzymes that are not present in humans and other animals. While humans and other animals make some amino acids, they do not have the enzyme EPSPS and, consequently, do not make the aromatic amino acids. As a result, these so-called essential amino acids must be present in our diet. Nor do we get our organic nitrogen from nitrate, as high nitrate levels are toxic to humans, especially infants. We get our nitrogen from organic compounds in our diet.

Keep in mind, however, that the same is not necessarily true of other herbicides. The common lawn weed killer 2,4-D, for example, is a chlorinated hydrocarbon, a family of highly reactive chemicals that are known to have nasty effects on human genes and metabolism. On the other hand, even though glyphosate and similar chemicals are considered relatively safe, common sense tells us to always treat all synthetic chemicals with caution.

Summary

The first step in producing a transgenic plant is to find the gene for a trait that you want to insert into the plant. There are several ways to obtain a gene. The first is to isolate messenger RNA and, using the enzyme reverse transcriptase, construct a complementary DNA (cDNA) library. Another method is to reverse engineer DNA, based on the amino acid sequence of the desired protein. A third method is to induce mutations by treating seeds with ionizing radiation or chemical mutagens.

Inserting the cloned gene—transforming plant cells—is accomplished by treating protoplasts (naked plant cells) with a brief pulse of electricity, by "shooting" the gene into protoplasts with a gene gun, or by enlisting the aid of nature's own genetic engineer, the crown gall bacterium (*Agrobacterium tumifasciens*).

Engineering herbicide tolerance in plants involves inserting genes that encode a less sensitive version of a critical enzyme or a gene that encodes a protein that deactivates the herbicide before it can interfere with a critical metabolic process.

6 Genetically Modified Plants
From Herbicides to Vaccines

...whoever could make two ears of corn, or two blades of grass, to grow upon a spot of ground where only one grew before, would do ... more essential service to his country, than the whole race of politicians put together.

—Jonathan Swift (1667–1745)
Anglo-Irish author of *Gulliver's Travels*

Genetically Modified Plants
From Herbicides to Vaccines

In the previous chapter, we saw how easily plants are transformed, so it may not be too surprising that most of the first genetically engineered products to enter the market involved agriculture. Crop plants engineered for resistance to herbicides, insects, and disease have been widely accepted by farmers around the world. Other plants have been engineered for enhanced food quality and nutrition. Anticipated products include crop plants better able to withstand the stresses of drought, flooding, salty soils, and low temperature. Also on the horizon are plants engineered as bioreactors to produce vaccines, plastics, and other useful consumer products.

HERBICIDE TOLERANCE

Herbicide tolerance was one of the first traits to be engineered in plants because it involves only a single gene and there appeared to be a ready market for the product. Glyphosate tolerance is a good example. Unlike most other herbicides, when glyphosate is sprayed on the leaves, it rapidly moves to the roots. Because it kills the roots as well as the aboveground portion of the plant, glyphosate is particularly effective against perennial plants, such as dandelions. This is one of the reasons for the immense popularity of glyphosate herbicides.

What is the value in having genetically modified herbicide-tolerant crops? The value in herbicide tolerance is most directly for the farmer. Left unattended, weeds reduce crop yields by $12 billion annually or more. Additional billions are spent every year attempting to control weeds. In normal practice, weed control involves several passes over the field with different herbicides because various weeds germinate at different times. But once the crop itself has germinated, spraying for weeds without damaging the crop plants themselves is tricky at best. Thus, the traditional approach requires complex mixtures of herbicides and multiple sprayings with a consequent heavy chemical load on the soil. When the crop plants themselves have the capacity to resist herbicides, the weeds can be killed with a single pass after the crop has emerged, without any lasting damage to the crop plants. The result is that less diesel fuel is consumed, fewer herbicides are sprayed on the fields, and the farmer's costs go down. A recent study by a British firm, for example, surveyed 18 countries and found that, by reducing the number of trips across the field for spraying, genetically modified crops have saved farmers 475 million gallons of fuel over the last nine years and reduced pesticide use by 14%. In the end, consumers benefit as well because of the reduction in greenhouse gas emissions and lower pesticide load on the environment.

The Mystery of White Petunias

Dr. Rich Jorgensen, a plant biologist at the University of Arizona, had the idea of using recombinant DNA to develop new colors in petunia flowers. In the original experiment, extra copies of the gene for purple pigment were inserted into petunia plants. The expectation was that the extra genes would cause the petals to make more pigment than normal and thus produce flowers with a more intense purple color. Unexpectedly, the transgenic plants produced white flowers instead!

Jorgensen eventually discovered that the inserted genes produced an unusual double-stranded messenger RNA rather than the single-stranded messenger RNA that plants normally produce. But remember that plant viruses are RNA viruses and their RNA happens to be double-stranded. Apparently, petunia plants have a mechanism that allows them to recognize viral RNA and destroy it. When the transgene produced double-stranded RNA, the cell apparently mistook it for virus RNA and set about destroying it. However, because the cell's own gene and the transgene produce RNA with the same base sequence, the plant's defense system could not discriminate between the two and the RNA produced by the normal gene was destroyed as well. The gene for purple color remained intact, but

(continued on page 88)

(continued from page 87)

the messenger RNA that it normally produces failed to accumulate. With no intact messenger RNA left in the cytoplasm, the cell was unable to make any of the purple pigment. Jorgenson called this phenomenon RNA interference (RNAi).

It did not take long for scientists to recognize that RNAi was not a property solely of plant cells but could be used to explain similar phenomena in organisms from nematodes (roundworms) to fruit flies to humans. These phenomena are now referred to more broadly as RNA silencing because they prevent the gene from being expressed. It appears that virtually any gene can be suppressed at will simply by knowing its DNA sequence and constructing the appropriate double-stranded RNA to trigger the "immune" response. RNAi and other RNA silencing techniques have great potential for treating diseases with a genetic component. RNAi therapy has been used successfully to treat diseases such as Huntington's disease, Lou Gehrig's disease, hepatitis, and breast cancer in mice and age-related macular degeneration causing loss of vision in humans. And it all started with transgenic petunias.

RESISTANCE TO INSECTS AND DISEASE

Weeds aren't the only problem faced by farmers—they must constantly fight insects and diseases caused by bacteria and fungi as well. Crop losses due to insects and plant diseases far exceed those of weeds, amounting to economic losses of more than $100 billion and significant losses in food production (Figure 6.1). Traditional insecticides are not the answer because they kill beneficial insects and crop pests equally well. Nowhere is this more obvious than in orchards across North America. Most orchard growers now find it necessary to import hives of bees during the pollinating season because natural bee populations have been decimated by years of widespread insecticide use. In fact, beekeeping is a growth industry as beekeepers follow the pollinating seasons from one crop to the next. Crops

Figure 6.1 A Colorado potato beetle feeds on its favorite food, a potato leaf. A major focus of the biotechnology industry is the creation of insecticides that will reduce the impact of destructive insects, such as the Colorado potato beetle.

engineered to control insects eating on plants could be beneficial because they would target only the insects that feed on the crop plants themselves. They could possibly even stimulate a resurgence in natural bee populations.

Genetic modifications to control insects exploit naturally occurring bacterial poisons called **enterotoxins** (from the Greek word *enteron* meaning "intestine"). Enterotoxins are toxic chemicals that act in the gut. One of the most common enterotoxins is the protein produced by *Bacillus thuringiensis* (Bt), a common soil bacterium. When the protein is ingested by the larvae of susceptible insects, the protein binds to receptors in the insect's gut and interferes with the absorption of nutrients. Sprays containing dried Bt bacteria have been used for several decades by organic gardeners as a way to control the Colorado potato beetle and other garden insect pests. But these products are expensive and they are rapidly inactivated in

Bt Corn and the Monarch Butterfly

You may have heard the claim that corn dusted with pollen from Bt corn could wipe out monarch butterflies. It began in 1999 when a group of researchers at Cornell University in New York State reported in the journal *Nature* the results of an experiment they conducted on feeding corn pollen to monarch larvae. After the monarchs migrate north in the summer, they lay their eggs on milkweed plants. When the larvae emerge, they feed on milkweed as their primary food source.

The Cornell group reported that larvae of the monarch butterfly grazing on milkweed dusted with pollen from Bt corn apparently suffered higher mortality than larvae grazing on milkweed dusted with non-Bt corn pollen. Should this be a surprise? Not really. The Bt protein is toxic to lepidopteran insects, and monarch butterflies are, after all, lepidopteran insects. However, this report was quickly picked up by the news media and promoted as evidence for an unexpected result indicating that genetic modification would have negative effects on the environment.

At issue is how the Cornell group's laboratory results extrapolate to the real world. As it turns out, the answer is not very well. Consider the following points:

• Farmers treat milkweed plants as weeds, so they are not generally found in the cornfields themselves.

• Although milkweed plants do occur in the vicinity of cornfields, many, if not most, milkweed plants that are potential hosts for monarch larvae are some distance from cornfields.

the field, so their use in large-scale agriculture is not practical. However, the gene that encodes for the Bt protein (the protein is called CryIAb) has been cloned into crops such as corn, cotton, and potatoes as an effective control against the European corn borer, cotton boll weevil, and Colorado potato beetle. The engi-

---

- Corn pollen does not travel well. Only 10% travels farther than 3 to 5 meters (9 to 15 feet) from the edge of the field.

- Corn pollen is normally shed over a period of 8 to 10 days. For the pollen to harm the monarch larvae, they would have to emerge and be feeding during that period. Typically, the feeding periods of monarch larvae do not coincide with pollen shed.

- Other studies have shown that for the pollen to be toxic to monarch larvae, the pollen density must be greater than 135 to 150 pollen grains per cm^2 of leaf surface. The average density on milkweed plants within 3 m (9 ft) of a corn field is only 20 to 30 grains per cm^2.

- The Cornell study itself indicated that, given the option, monarch larvae prefer to graze on leaves that are free of corn pollen. If a larva encounters a pollen-coated leaf, it will usually avoid it and move on.

- It is now possible to control the expression of genes in specific tissues, and new genetically modified lines that produce the Bt toxin in leaves, but not in the pollen, are coming available.

Does Bt corn pollen place monarch butterflies at risk? Based on all of the available evidence, it seems that the risk to monarch butterflies in the wild is virtually nil. This illustrates the fear with which many people approach genetic modification and how one should not jump to conclusions until all the facts are in.

neered crops don't need to be sprayed with insecticides because plants that carry the gene make the protein and the insects ingest the protein as they graze. Beneficial insects and others that don't graze on the engineered plants are not affected.

Genetic engineering has also proven successful in protecting plants against fungi and viruses. Chitin is a major constituent of fungal cell walls. Many plants, when invaded by fungi, produce chitinase, an enzyme that degrades chitin and prevents further growth of the fungus. Plants engineered to produce chitinase as a normal constituent exhibit increased resistance to infection by fungal pathogens. In the case of viruses, it appears possible to actually "vaccinate" plants against virus infections by transforming the plant with a cDNA clone for the virus coat protein. How the presence of the coat protein in the cell invokes immunity is not known, but the strategy has proven successful for several crops, including tobacco, tomato, alfalfa, and rice.

ENGINEERING FOR ENHANCED PRODUCTIVITY AND NUTRITION

Herbicide tolerance was one of the first genetic modifications to come onto the market for the simple reason that it was a straightforward trait that involved only a single gene. Many other desirable plant traits are more difficult to engineer because they involve multiple genes. For example, one "holy grail" for plant breeders and biotechnologists alike is to increase the total amount of carbon that ends up in the leaves and seeds of traditional crop plants due to photosynthesis. The amount of carbon accumulated by the plant, called productivity, is one of the keys to increasing food production for an ever-expanding world population. It may sound relatively simple, but increasing productivity through biotechnology is more easily said than done. Productivity is a complicated process, dependent on the balance between the amount of carbon taken up through photosynthesis and the amount of carbon lost through respiration. Both photosynthesis and respiration are governed by a large number of genes that interact with each other in complex ways. The bottom line is that any improvements to plant productivity through biotechnology are not likely to be achieved until scientists understand much more about which genes are involved and how these complex pathways interact.

Changing the oils in seeds, however, is another story. The production of oilseed crops such as canola, safflower, and sunflower is a large component of the North American agricultural economy. These oils are used extensively as cooking and salad oils and in manufactured food products. One popular source of oil is rapeseed, a collection of *Brassica* species in the mustard family. The oils of native rapeseed, however, contain high amounts of glucosinolates and erucic acid. Glucosinolates are organic sulfur compounds that are easily converted to mustard oils, flavor constituents that give the pungent taste to mustard and horseradish as well as the distinctive flavors of other members of the same family, such as cabbage, broccoli, and cauliflower. If that is not enough to discourage the use of rapeseed oil, the erucic acid content adds its own distinctively unpleasant taste. Almost all the world's rapeseed oil now comes from a single line of rapeseed in which the content of both glucosinolate and erucic acid has been reduced to virtually zero. Known commercially as canola, this rapeseed was developed in Canada not by genetic modification, but by traditional plant breeding.

Scientists are now looking to recombinant DNA techniques in order to further improve canola and other oilseed crops. One objective, of course, is to simply increase the yield of oil. This might be accomplished by engineering overexpression of certain enzymes involved in the biosynthesis of oils. Another objective is to change the fatty acid composition of plant oils to better match different food or industrial applications (Table 6.1). For example, unsaturated fatty acids are considered healthier than saturated fatty acids, so engineering plants to produce oils with a higher proportion of unsaturated fatty acids for use in cooking and salad oils would benefit health-conscious consumers. Soybean, canola, and flax have all been engineered to produce more polyunsaturated and fewer saturated fatty acids. On the other hand, oils with a higher proportion of stearic acid (a natural saturated fatty acid) could be used to solidify margarine and shortenings at room temperature. This would bypass the need for hydrogenation and the associated generation of unhealthy trans fats.

The development of golden rice is one of the greatest biotech success stories. While North Americans and Europeans tend to favor potatoes, white rice is the staple food throughout much of

Table 6.1   Fatty Acid Composition of Common Plant and Animal Fats and Oils

Fatty Acid (% of total lipid)

Oil	Saturated	Unsaturated	Ratio (Unsaturated/ Saturated
Safflower oil	8	87	10.9
Corn oil	11	85	7.7
Olive oil	11	84	7.6
Soybean oil	15	79	5.3
Peanut oil	18	76	4.2
Margarine	26	70	2.7
Fish	15	78	5.2
Beef fat	48	47	1.0
Butter	55	39	0.7

Fatty Acids and the Trans-fat Problem

Plant fats and oils belong to a large and diverse group of molecules called lipids. Lipids are molecules that are soluble in lipid solvents. This may be a confusing bit of circular reasoning, but it does emphasize that lipids share an aversion to water (hydrophobic). Fats and oils have a similar chemical composition; the only difference is that fats are solid at room temperature and oils are liquid.

The principal components of fats and oils in plants are triglycerides, in which three long-chain fatty acids are attached to a three-carbon alcohol, glycerol. Fatty acids are long chains of carbon and hydrogen atoms containing anywhere from 8 to 22 carbon atoms with an acid group (called a carboxyl group) at one end. A fatty acid is referred to as either saturated or unsaturated, depending on the number of hydrogen atoms it contains. A fatty acid is considered saturated when all of the hydrogen-binding sites are filled and unsaturated when one or more pairs of hydrogen atoms are missing. Where a pair of hydrogen atoms is missing, an extra bond (a carbon-carbon double bond) forms between the two carbon atoms. A fatty acid with more than one double bond is often referred to as polyunsaturated.

The key to the composition of fats and oils lies in the fatty acid mix that makes up the triglyceride. Saturated fatty acids, for example, have a higher melting point than unsaturated fatty acids. Thus, a triglyceride made up of two or three saturated fatty acids will be solid at room temperature—a fat—while oils have a high proportion of unsaturated fatty acids. Another interesting feature of the double bond is that it can occur in two configurations called *cis* and *trans*. In the fatty acids that occur naturally in plants, the double bond is always in the *cis* configuration. When margarine and shortening, both fats, are manufactured from plant oils, the oils are cooked in the presence of hydrogen at high temperature and under pressure. This process, called hydrogenation, "saturates" some of the double bonds in order to give the product the required melting properties. Unfortunately, hydrogenation also converts some of the *cis* double bonds to *trans* double bonds, or trans fats. Trans fats have lately been linked to heart disease and other human health problems.

the world. Unfortunately, polished white rice does not contain any of the orange pigment beta-carotene, a pro-vitamin that the body converts to vitamin A. Vitamin A deficiency, which leads to blindness, especially in young children, is a chronic problem throughout much of Southeast Asia and other parts of the developing world. Rice does, however, produce a precursor to vitamin A. A team of Swiss and German scientists successfully modified rice, using genes from daffodils, to convert the precursor to beta-carotene. The transgenic rice is known as golden rice because of the color imparted by the accumulated beta-carotene. The team was also able to add additional genes that increased the iron content of rice, potentially reducing the incidence of iron deficiency that affects an estimated 3.7 billion people worldwide. Golden rice differs from most GMOs in that it was developed with the assistance of philanthropic and government agencies rather than private multinational companies and has been made freely available to rice breeders and growers.

Nutritional deficiencies can affect farm animals as well. Of the 20 amino acids that go into making protein, 8 of them are synthesized only in microorganisms and plants. These are the essential amino acids, mentioned earlier in chapter 5, that must be included in the diet of all vertebrates. Corn is a popular feed for livestock such as cattle, hogs, and poultry, but corn protein contains exceptionally low amounts of the essential amino acid lysine. Lysine is expensive to produce, and it is estimated that the livestock feed industry purchases $1 billion worth of lysine every year to supplement animal feeds. High-lysine corn varieties have been available through conventional breeding for more than 30 years, but yields were too low to be profitable. One biotech company has genetically modified high-yielding varieties of corn for high lysine content and is expected to bring the new varieties into commercial production by 2007 or 2008.

MOLECULAR FARMING

Plants make a lot of strange chemicals. In most plants, a significant proportion of their assimilated carbon and energy is diverted to the synthesis of molecules that have no obvious role in their growth and development. Many of these molecules have found use in antiquity as folk remedies, soaps, and essences. Others have found use as dyestuffs and feedstocks for chemical industries (gums, resins, rubber, and others) and even more have found use as therapeutic drugs. Even though the recent trend has been toward chemical synthesis of drugs designed to target specific illnesses more effectively, plants traditionally have been the principal source of therapeutic drugs. With the advent of rDNA technology, however, plants are being viewed as production vehicles with the potential to not only stock your local pharmacy but to produce a variety of other useful molecules as well.

Using transgenic plants as bioreactors to produce useful molecules is called **molecular farming** (Figure 6.2) Because many of these molecules are intended to have use as therapeutic drugs (or pharmaceuticals), the technique is often referred to as "molecular pharming." Most of the therapeutic products produced in transgenic plants are proteins, such as antibodies and antigens or vaccines—products that have previously been extracted directly from other animals, cultured in chicken eggs, or simply not produced at all.

Why engineer plants to produce these products? The answer is that traditional methods are very costly. Plants, on the other hand, are easily transformed and they can produce huge quantities of soluble protein at relatively low cost. Among plants that are being used for molecular pharming are alfalfa, bananas, carrots, potatoes, and tomatoes. One of the favored crops for molecular pharming, however, is tobacco. Tobacco is one of the easiest plants to transform, it produces a large leaf mass, and, perhaps most important, it is a non-food crop. The significance of this last attribute will be addressed in chapter 7. And the

Figure 6.2 A researcher inoculates a plant with an engineered virus that produces proteins for human therapeutic use. This technique is often used in molecular farming, also known as molecular pharming.

purified pharmaceuticals are not contaminated with nicotine or any other nasty tobacco chemicals.

Pioneering work in molecular pharming has been carried out in the laboratory of C. J. Arntzen, a plant biologist at Arizona State University. Arntzen began his work in the mid-1980s and by 1992 had cloned the gene for an antigen of the hepatitis B virus into tobacco. An antigen is a protein that stimulates the body's immune cells to produce antibodies that fight off invading organisms. Arntzen's group showed that the antigens isolated from the transgenic plants did indeed invoke an immune response when injected into mice.

But Arntzen was primarily interested in developing a plant-based system for producing low-cost vaccines that could be used to immunize people in developing countries. These are countries where high cost and logistical problems such as lack of transportation, trained medical personnel, and refrigeration can thwart conventional vaccination programs. Arntzen believed that a more cost-effective method would be an oral vaccine that could be delivered in a locally grown food product. So, he switched from tobacco to potatoes and showed that the cloned hepatitis B antigens could also stimulate an immune response simply by feeding the potatoes to mice. They had successfully produced an oral vaccine! Prior to this, the only successful oral vaccine has been the oral polio vaccine, and polio has been effectively eradicated worldwide.

Arntzen and his group also successfully cloned into potatoes the genes for the toxin produced by the bacterium *Escherichia coli* (*E. coli*) and the coat protein for the Norwalk virus. Both *E. coli* and the Norwalk virus are common agents for severe diarrhea in humans and are a serious problem in developing countries. The transgenic potatoes were also successful in invoking immune responses in mice, so, in 1998, the first human trials were conducted. Eleven volunteers were fed potatoes transformed with the *E. coli* antigen with positive results: 10 volunteers showed a fourfold increase in serum antibodies and 6 showed a fourfold increase in intestinal antibodies as well. The results of this trial clearly illustrated the potential for transgenic plants to be used as production vehicles for **edible vaccines**. In 2001, the cost of injecting a patient in remote areas with a conventional vaccine was estimated to be about $120. The estimated cost for delivery of an edible vaccine was as low as $0.02.

There is, however, one problem with using potatoes as a vaccine delivery vehicle. They must be eaten raw. Cooking, unfortunately, denatures the protein and renders it inactive. While mice may not object to eating raw potatoes, most humans do, especially those in countries where potatoes are not a normal part of the diet. It is likely that other, more palatable plant sources, such as bananas or tomatoes, would be more acceptable.

In the meantime, scientists around the world were getting into molecular pharming. In fact, by 2002, there were an estimated 400 plant-derived genetically engineered pharmaceutical products (drugs and vaccines) in clinical development in the United States and Canada alone. One example is an Australian group that has cloned the gene for measles vaccine into tobacco. They are now trying to clone the gene into rice. Measles is responsible for almost a million deaths each year and they hope that mixing transgenic rice flour with breast milk will be a simple and inexpensive way to vaccinate children in poor, remote communities.

Although production of therapeutic proteins is an important step forward and captures the imagination, molecular farming is in no way limited to pharmaceuticals. One of the more interesting applications is the production of biodegradable plastics. Although corn oil has long been used as a substitute for petroleum in the manufacture of traditional plastics, the product is no more biodegradable than those made from petroleum. On the other hand, there are many species of bacteria that naturally produce fully biodegradable plastics known by the somewhat daunting name of **polyhydroxyalkanoates (PHAs)**. In bacterial cells, the plastic accumulates as large bodies or inclusions, apparently as a means for storing carbon, in much the same way that plant cells store carbon as starch and animals store carbon as glycogen. Plants could also be used to produce these plastics. PHAs are synthesized from a metabolic intermediate, called **acetyl-CoA**, that is found in virtually all cells. Acetyl-CoA is also the primary building block for fats and oils, so plants produce it in fairly large

Figure 6.3 The cotton plant is a promising candidate for future genetic engineering. By altering the genes of the cotton plant, scientists may be able to produce a cotton fiber that has qualities superior to non-genetically engineered cotton fiber.

amounts. Recently, the enzymes necessary to produce PHAs have been cloned into *Arabidopsis* (a favorite experimental plant for plant biologists) and the transgenic plants accumulated PHA inclusions virtually identical to those found in the bacteria.

One plant that has interesting possibilities is cotton (*Gossypium hirsutum*) (Figure 6.3). In genetically engineered cotton plants, the genes for biodegradable plastics were expressed in the seed hair (fiber) cells. The amount of PHA (in this case, polyhydroxybutarate, or PHB) produced was not large, but it was enough to alter the thermal properties of the cotton fiber. The transgenic fibers conducted less heat than normal fibers, suggesting that transgenic fibers could have enhanced insulation properties. One of these winters you just might be wearing clothing made from a cotton-polyester blend harvested directly from the cotton field!

Where is the value in engineering plants to produce plastic? As you know, plastics are a mainstay of our modern consumer economy and because of that they also represent about one-fifth of the municipal waste across North America. The plastics made from petroleum do not break down very readily. Some biodegradable PHAs are currently being produced by bacterial fermentation, but fermentation requires large industrial facilities and consumes substantial amounts of energy. Producing biodegradable plastics by fermentation is currently about five times more expensive than the cost of conventional plastics made from petroleum. Plants, on the other hand, which are known for producing large quantities of products such as starch and oils, might also be adapted to produce PHAs on a commercial scale. Since there are many bacteria capable of using PHAs as a carbon source, PHA-based consumer products discarded into landfills would be 100% biodegradable. This would be a real benefit for the environment.

Summary

The first generation of genetically modified plants has focused on herbicide tolerance and resistance to insects and disease. The primary beneficiaries of these products are the farmers, who benefit by reduced production costs. Consumers benefit indirectly by the reduction of greenhouse gas emissions from farming operations and lowered pesticide load in the environment.

Another objective of using rDNA in plant breeding is to produce plants with enhanced nutrition. The improvement of quantity and composition of oils from oilseed crops is one area under development. It may be possible to change the oil composition to serve particular needs. For example, increasing the proportion of stearic acid in plant oils could help to solidify shortenings at room temperature. This would avoid the need to hydrogenate oils, a process that creates unhealthy trans fats. Golden rice is another example of a genetically modified plant with improved nutrition that could benefit young people in parts of the world where rice is a staple product.

Molecular farming is the use of plants as bioreactors to produce a variety of useful molecules. The primary focus is presently on using plants to produce vaccines and other protein-based pharmaceutical products. Producing edible vaccines in plants would drastically lower the cost of delivery and improve access to immunizations in the developing world. It may also be possible to engineer plants to produce biodegradable plastics and other useful products.

7 Putting Genetically Modified Organisms in Perspective

Every business and every product has risks. You can't get around it.
—Lee Iacocca (1924–)
American business executive

Putting Genetically Modified Organisms in Perspective

Perhaps you have seen them in the news—anti-GMO protesters dressed like a cob of corn or a tomato with a fish head. GMO supporters might be tempted to laugh at such antics, but it is important to remember that genetic modification (GM) is a new technology. There are, no doubt, some protesters who are simply "anti" new technology, but for others there are legitimate concerns about the safety of the food they eat and the impact this new technology may have on their lives and the environment (Figure 7.1).

Most consumers accept without question foods produced through what is now called **conventional plant breeding**. Such foods are considered natural, safe, and acceptable. Many feel that GMOs, however, are not natural, safe, or acceptable. GMOs should be vigorously debated, as the product of any new technology should be, but the debate must be based on an informed understanding of the facts. The debate should not be distorted by scientific misinformation and misinterpretation or, worse yet, personal invective or political objectives. Informed debate on the GMO issue can only come about when the public has a broader understanding of the underlying scientific foundation.

You should now be able to appreciate that the scientific concepts behind genetically modified foods are not all that difficult to comprehend. But how does rDNA technology stack up against traditional plant breeding? Are GM foods any more or less safe to eat than conventionally bred foods? Are GMOs potentially harmful to the environment? Are there real benefits to GM foods and other products for consumers in North America as well as in developing nations?

CONVENTIONAL PLANT BREEDING

We can be quite certain that someone who says that they prefer "natural" foods does not have in mind going back to collecting nuts and berries as their distant ancestors once did. What this statement usually implies is that they do not want some scientist

Figure 7.1 A Greenpeace activist wears a mask and shows a hand full of peas in front of the European Council building in Brussels, Belgium. Worldwide, many organizations are calling for governments to restrict or ban the sale of GMOs and GM-foods out of concern over the safety of these products.

or large multinational company "messing" with their food. But how natural is "natural"?

The truth is that humans have been "messing around" with their food for a very long time. We have, in fact, been practicing genetic modification since the dawn of agriculture some 10,000 years ago. The wheat that goes into your bread and breakfast cereal is the product of three different species, and the hybrid corn of today bears little resemblance to its ancestor (a some-what scrawny tropical grass called teosinte). Gene transfer by *Agrobacterium* is not limited to the laboratory: *A. tumifascium* is a common soil bacterium that goes about subtly transform-ing plants on a daily basis. We have all occasionally, if unknow-ingly, consumed these naturally occurring GMOs for as long as humans have been eating plants. Along the way, humans began cross-breeding plants to combine traits and produce crops such as pumpkins, potatoes, oats, rice, tomatoes, and other food plants that probably would not have existed as we know them without human intervention.

Conventional plant breeding begins with **selection**. A farmer selects the biggest and best of each year's crop and reserves it for use as seed for the following year. Farmers are practicing a form of Darwinian evolution, because selection slowly changes the characteristics of the plant until they may no longer resemble the original plant—yields are higher and the fruit is larger, sweeter, and tastier. Corn is an excellent example. Under the influence of human selection, the short floral head of the tropical grass teosinte, with one or two rows of small seeds, has become the modern version of sweet corn with a "cob" 8 to 10 inches long and 16 to 18 rows of sweet-tasting fruits.

Over time, selection was combined with crossing. Unwilling to leave the development of foods to the whims of nature, early farm-ers (the first plant breeders) began transferring pollen from one plant with superior characteristics to the pistil of another superior plant. The hope was that at least some of the resulting offspring, called **hybrids,** would possess the best traits of each parent. Mar-quis wheat, until recently the world standard for breadmaking quality, was developed in the early 1900s by crossing other wheat varieties and carefully selecting for the best breadmaking seeds.

Hybridization has been developed to a fine art by modern corn breeders. Hybrid corn is produced by crossing two or more **inbred lines.** An inbred line is a genetically uniform variety of plant that produces "true" by seed. In other words, the seeds from successive generations can be planted with no significant changes in their characteristics. Most hybrid corn seed sold to farmers today is actually double cross seed produced from four inbred lines (Figure 7.2). Hybridization has brought many new vegetable cultivars (varieties under cultivation) to farmers and gardeners. In addition to corn, hybrid vegetables include tomatoes, melons, cucumbers, cabbage, carrots, onions, cauliflower, broccoli, peppers, and squash.

Before hybrid crops appeared on the scene, farmers grew **open-pollinated** cultivars and traditionally saved a portion of the grain from the current crop to use as their seed for the next season. In many cases, the farmers continued to select, perhaps inadvertently, each time they saved seed. Over time, this practice gave rise to local populations that were genetically suited to the microclimate of a particular farm. These populations are called **landraces,** referring to a "breed" or "race" that is highly adapted to local conditions. One of the criticisms of GM crops is that they are patented, and farmers, in their contract with the seed producer, are prohibited from saving seed. However, most conventional hybrids do not breed "true," so new hybrid seed must also be purchased each year as well or the performance of the crop deteriorates. While both conventional hybrids and GM crops have led to increased yields, they both also tend to decrease genetic variability through the loss of landraces. In either case, the farmer must weigh the advantages of higher yields against cost and any other disadvantages. In recent years, numerous far-sighted organizations have sprung up with the purpose of maintaining open pollinated "heritage" varieties of vegetables, such as tomatoes, in order to preserve genetic diversity.

One disadvantage of crossing as a breeding technique is that each parent in a cross contributes 50% of the genes. For example, suppose you want to improve the disease resistance of a cultivar of superior bread wheat by crossing it with a wild relative that has a much higher disease resistance. Not only does the wild relative provide the desired disease resistance gene, but there are another

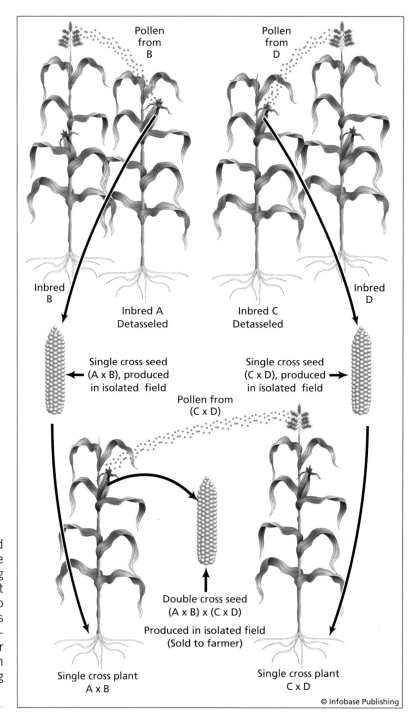

Pollen from B

Pollen from D

Inbred B

Inbred A Detasseled

Inbred C Detasseled

Inbred D

Single cross seed (A x B), produced in isolated field

Single cross seed (C x D), produced in isolated field

Pollen from (C x D)

Double cross seed (A x B) x (C x D)

Produced in isolated field (Sold to farmer)

Single cross plant A x B

Single cross plant C x D

Figure 7.2
Double cross seed is produced by the careful breeding of four different inbred lines. Two of the inbred lines must be detasseled in order to prevent them from pollinating themselves.

25,000 or more genes that come along for the ride. Many of these genes may be undesirable—they may cause the stem to grow long and weak, reduce the yield, or lower the quality of the flour.

A large amount of the conventional breeder's effort is spent simply getting rid of this genetic garbage. This is usually accomplished by crossing the hybrid back to the original commercial cultivar, a process called **backcrossing**. This means that all of the progeny, which may number in the thousands, must be carefully screened and those with undesirable traits discarded. The remaining progeny are again backcrossed to the original cultivar. This screening-selection-backcrossing routine is repeated generation after generation until the breeder is at last convinced that he has eliminated the undesirable traits and has regenerated the superior bread wheat with the single addition of the desired disease resistance gene. It may take 10–12 generations—meaning 10–12 years—to eliminate the undesirable genes. Even then, the new commercial strain will still be contaminated with unknown foreign genes contributed by the wild relative. It is impractical, if not impossible, to remove them all.

One advantage cited by proponents of GM crops is that producing a transgenic "hybrid" is far more precise. Recombinant DNA technology allows the breeder to select a single gene and insert *only that gene* into the genome of the commercial cultivar. The resulting progeny are then identical to the parent with the exception of that one additional gene. There are no undesirable or unknown genes carried along, and the new cultivar with the new trait can be available to growers within two to three years.

DEVELOPING NEW TRAITS FOR THE CONVENTIONAL BREEDER

Suppose you are a plant breeder and would like to introduce a new trait, but you are unable to find a compatible wild type or other plant with that particular trait. If you don't want to resort to rDNA technology, what are your options? A conventional plant breeder actually has a variety of methods for creating the gene for a trait of interest. Earlier, in chapter 5, we mentioned the use of mutations to generate new traits. Let's use wheat as an example and see how mutations can be used to advantage.

Traditional wheat varieties carry their grain at the top of long stems. As breeders succeeded in producing plants with larger numbers of heavier grains, the plants developed a tendency to fall over and lie on the ground. This is known as lodging, a condition commonly precipitated by heavy rains or winds (Figure 7.3). Lodged plants are a real problem for the farmer. They are more difficult to harvest, and the grains, now in contact with the ground, are more susceptible to losses from soil-dwelling insects, fungi, and bacteria. What is the solution to this problem? Well, if you have ever tried to break a pencil you must know that a stubby pencil is much more difficult to break than a long pencil of the same diameter. The same is true of plant stems, so one solution to the lodging problem would be a wheat plant with a shorter stem. Great idea, but how do you go about it?

In most cases, stem length is regulated by a natural plant hormone called gibberellin. Plants that make less of the hormone generally have shorter stems. In fact, genetic dwarfs with reduced gibberellin levels are quite common in nature. Bush beans or peas, for example, are shorter than their "tall" vinelike climbing relatives simply because they make less gibberellin. Thus, one way to create a dwarf plant is to induce a mutation that reduces gibberellin levels. Mutated seedlings can be screened for a desired trait such as shortened stem length. Those seedlings are then introduced into a conventional breeding program. **Mutation breeding** is a common technique in conventional breeding. Over the last half of the 1900s, more than 1,400 cultivars, including several short-stemmed wheat and rice cultivars, have been developed through induced mutations. These varieties are accepted as "natural" foods solely because they are not GMOs.

A variety of other techniques for manipulating genes are also available to the conventional breeder. **Embryo rescue** is a

Figure 7.3 The toppling of plants before harvest is known as lodging. These corn plants became lodged after the roots of the plants were damaged by insects.

technique used to mate two plants, often from different species, that would not normally mate in nature. The resulting embryos do not often survive naturally, but can be removed (or "rescued") from the ovary and encouraged to reproductive maturity by culturing them artificially. Haploid breeding is a method in which pollen or egg cells, which normally have only one set of chromosomes, are treated with chemicals that force them to make a copy of their own chromosomes. The cells, which now have two exact copies of every gene, can be induced to form plantlets in tissue culture and grown to sexual maturity.

Finally, when plants are cloned by micropropagation, there are often odd plantlets that arise apparently by spontaneous genetic changes (that is, by mutation) in the vegetative cells. To the micropropagationist, these "sports" are simply defective plants to be discarded. Others, however, have recognized that these genetic changes, now called **somoclonal variation** (**SCV**), might be sources of new and useful traits. SCV has been exploited to improve growth habit, maturity date, and tuber characteristics in potatoes. In fact, the popular Russet Burbank variety of potato arose as a somaclonal variant of the original Burbank variety.

As intrusive as mutational breeding and these other techniques may sound, they illustrate the extent to which conventional plant breeding involves genetic modification but without involving rDNA techniques.

FOOD SAFETY: WOULD YOU EAT DNA?

An increasing concern of most consumers is food safety and whether genetic modification by rDNA techniques compromises that safety. But in what way could rDNA techniques compromise food safety? Would it be the "new" or "foreign" DNA that is introduced or would it be the "new" protein encoded by that DNA? And, for comparison, can we evaluate the safety of conventional foods?

First, let's address the question of "foreign" DNA and proteins. In his book *Pandora's Picnic Basket*, Alan McHughen relates an anecdote about an anti-GMO activist who stormed out of a meeting declaring that "You'll never convince me to eat DNA." A recent survey indicated that a surprising percentage of the public believe that natural foods do not contain DNA but that GMOs do. All of the foods we eat contain DNA because DNA is a constituent of all living cells. Only highly processed foods such as soy protein, refined cooking and salad oils, and similar products do not contain significant amounts of DNA, but even those might contain traces. Many natural foods such as buttermilk and yogurt also contain cultures of harmless bacteria. You can't avoid bacteria—they are everywhere in our environment. We take steps such as pasteurizing milk to destroy harmful bacteria in the food we eat, but the bacteria are still there; they are just dead. So, our diets contain a fair amount of bacterial

Fish Genes and GMO Myths

At the beginning of this chapter, we mentioned anti-GMO activists who dress as tomatoes with fish heads. This costume is based on the belief that tomatoes were engineered with genes from a fish, specifically arctic flounder. This is one of the myths of GMOs that arose probably out of a misinterpretation by an overzealous and non-critical reporter.

GM tomatoes were the first GMO vegetable to be released for human consumption in the early 1980s, but they were not modified with fish genes. The tomato, called the Flavr-Savr™, was engineered to delay softening and prolong shelf life while continuing to develop normal color and flavor. It was accomplished by removing a tomato gene—one that codes for the enzyme that causes the tissue to soften—and reinserting it backwards. The inverted gene could not be read by the cell's genetic machinery any better than you could read this sentence if it were printed backwards. (!ees dna flesruoy ti yrT) The engineered tomato made less of the softening enzyme and the shelf life of the tomato was prolonged.

Another unrelated idea being kicked around at the same time was that of transferring an anti-freeze gene from the Artic flounder to a crop plant. The idea was that this gene, which encodes an anti-freeze protein that helps the fish to survive in icy waters, would also help crop plants survive unseasonable frosts. In writing the story, the reporter apparently combined the Flavr-Savr™ project with the anti-freeze concept. Although the story has been thoroughly discredited, it has persisted with a life of its own.

The flounder gene idea was eventually tried—with strawberries, not tomatoes—and it didn't work. This should not be too surprising since fish and plants are very different organisms. They live in very different worlds and what works in one will not necessarily work in the other. Moreover, recent research has shown that winter strains of rye and other plants make their own anti-freeze proteins, so it is not necessary to look to fish genes for frost protection in plants.

DNA as well. We also eat lots of protein in the form of enzymes and structural proteins in our food. But cooking denatures both DNA and protein. DNA and protein are further denatured by the acids in our stomachs, and intestinal enzymes break down these molecules into their basic building blocks, which are absorbed into the bloodstream. These DNA and protein building blocks are the same regardless of whether they came from plants, animals, or bacteria.

Some people express concern about eating a "pesticide" or "toxin" when corn or potatoes are transformed with the gene that encodes Bt protein. Remember that Bt protein is toxic only to the larval stage of insects in the family Lepidoptera. It kills the larva by interfering with the absorption of nutrients in the gut. Bt protein does not affect humans, however, because the human gut is fundamentally different from the insect gut. The human gut does not have the receptors that are attacked by Bt protein, and the strongly acidic environment of the human gut immediately denatures the protein. The protein is then digested as any other protein is. Keep in mind as well that Bt is an approved insecticide for organic gardening. Finally, what is "foreign" DNA anyway? You might be aware that recent research has shown that humans share as much as 70% of their genes (and hence DNA) with earthworms and more than 95% with mice!

GM foods are not immune to safety and security problems, but neither are conventional foods. After all, plants have had billions of years to develop toxins that discourage creatures such as us from eating them. For example, the seeds (but thankfully not the fruit) of apples, cherries, and apricots, as well as some strains of lima beans, contain **cyanogenic glycosides.** These are chemical compounds that release cyanide when the cells are disrupted. The odd apple seed eaten with a core will probably cause little harm, but a half cup of dried seeds releases enough cyanide to kill an adult. Potatoes and tomatoes are in the same family as belladonna, deadly nightshade, and *Datura* (jimson weed), all of which contain deadly **alkaloids.** The potato alkaloid solanine accumulates in the green plants but not in the potato tubers themselves. However, potatoes that have turned green following exposure to strong light will contain elevated levels of solanine, which is why you should avoid eating green potatoes.

Numerous other foods contain various toxins as well. Here are just a few examples of toxins that are natural constituents of common foods:

- Banana peels and, to a lesser extent, the pulp, contain serotonin and other chemicals that raise blood pressure in animals.

- Kidney beans, soybeans, and peas contain lectins, molecules that cause red blood cells to clump and in large doses can interfere with the body's immune system.

- *Brassicas* (broccoli, brussels sprouts, cauliflower, cabbage, and others) contain glucosinolates (mustard oils) that are responsible for the pungent taste of these vegetables. Glucosinolates are also called goitrogens because they can interfere with iodine uptake by the thyroid gland, resulting in goiters (an enlargement of the thyroid gland). This is not a concern if the diet contains sufficient iodine.

- Coffee contains caffeine, an alkaloid that is toxic to the central nervous system.

- Papaya and pineapple contain proteolytic enzymes (enzymes that break down proteins) that will cause irritation of the mouth's mucous membranes.

- Aside from allergenic protein that can lead to anaphylactic shock in sensitive individuals, peanuts can become contaminated with molds that produce deadly aflatoxins.

This is not intended to put you off from eating fruits and vegetables. What you have to remember is that, except in rare circumstances, *the concentrations of toxins in common food plants are so low that they can be tolerated without ill effects*. We have also learned to avoid eating plants or parts of plants that produce unacceptably high levels of toxins. The point is that some plants do make things that are not necessarily good for you. We assume a certain level of risk when we eat these foods, but we have learned that the nutritional value of fruits and vegetables far outweighs the risk of death by starvation. The risk is manageable, so we do not use it as an excuse to stop eating fruits and vegetables.

Is it possible to create a toxic food by genetic modification? Of course it is, but the same is true of conventionally bred foods. A while back, for example, a new strain of potato produced by conventional breeding was found to have unacceptably high levels of solanine and had to be pulled from the market. There are two factors that help mitigate any concerns about food safety, not only for GMOs but for conventional foods as well. First, it is unlikely that any company would knowingly release an unsafe food, regardless of its origin, into the marketplace. The attendant publicity would likely be the death knell for the company and that is not what investors in those companies want. The second factor is that, at least in North America, new crop varieties are subjected to the scrutiny of several government agencies—the U.S. Department of Agriculture (USDA) and the Food and Drug Administration (FDA) in the United States and the Canadian Food Inspection Agency (CFIA) in Canada. In general, any new crop variety, whether produced by GM or conventional plant breeding, must meet three criteria before it can be registered and approved for release: it must be genetically distinct from other approved varieties, it must be genetically stable, and the new variety must produce a uniform population of plants. In addition, both GMOs and conventionally bred foods are carefully scrutinized to ensure that they are no more dangerous, especially with respect to allergenic and toxic properties, than the food they replace.

Some opponents of GMOs insist that no transgenic plant should be released until it is proven safe. This is called the precautionary principle. Is this a reasonable approach? Can you anticipate or test for every possible eventuality? Probably not. However, after more than 25 years of experimentation, there have been no unpredicted results from the release of any genetically modified product. Moreover, the USDA has reported that in 2002 American farmers planted nearly 80 million acres of genetically modified corn and soybeans. That acreage is without doubt much higher at this time and there have been no ill effects reported.

WHAT ABOUT THE ENVIRONMENT?

Beyond food safety, there appears to be some concern that GM plants might have an adverse impact on the environment. What kind of an impact might be expected? The principal concern appears to be that pesticide-resistant genes could spread into wild populations, creating a race of super weeds. Is this a valid concern?

The spread of genes could happen in two ways: GM plants could transfer genes by pollinating close relatives in the wild or they might "escape" and establish themselves outside cultivated plots. Most of the "first generation" GMOs are pesticide-resistant and should such a plant or gene escape into the wild, it is not likely to be a major problem. Why? A plant can succeed in the wild only when it enjoys some advantage over its competitors. An herbicide-resistant plant, for example, would enjoy no competitive advantage because it would not be challenged with herbicide. Even if it were necessary to use herbicide, a glyphosate-resistant plant could be killed with any one of several other herbicides. In addition, we know that resistance to herbicides arises naturally in wild and weed populations based on selection pressure. Finally, pesticide-resistant plants have been produced by conventional breeding, but no one seems unduly concerned about their release. If pesticide resistance is a problem, should it matter whether that resistance has been produced by rDNA techniques or by conventional breeding?

There might be some reason to be concerned about second-generation GMOs, however. These include traits such as cold tolerance or fungal resistance—traits that have yet to be developed.

In this case, escaped plants could suddenly acquire an adaptive advantage that could be exploited if a sudden cold snap, for example, killed off the competition. Another concern is molecular pharming: Plants that are used as bioreactors to make pharmaceuticals are clearly not intended for widespread environmental release or commodity food markets and must be carefully isolated to ensure there is no gene transfer to food crops.

If there is a final lesson when it comes to using this new technology, it is this: if there are going to be problems with food safety or the environment, they will arise because of the nature of the

A Tale of Two Wheats

In 2004, the U.S.-based chemical company Monsanto announced plans to seek permission for the release of a genetically modified, herbicide-tolerant wheat variety into the Canadian market. The wheat was modified by inserting a gene from a soil bacterium, and it would be tolerant to Monsanto's very popular herbicide, glyphosate. The announcement was met with vocal resistance from consumer groups, environmentalists, and farmers themselves. Consumer groups were concerned about the release of yet another GMO and corporate control over a major crop. Environmentalists were concerned that the "foreign" gene would spread into native grasses, and farmers who wanted to continue growing conventional wheat feared contamination of their crops with wind-spread pollen. Even the Canadian wheat marketing board expressed opposition, fearing the loss of European and other markets where the import of GMOs has been banned. Fearing a public relations disaster, Monsanto wisely decided to cancel its plans.

Meanwhile, thousands of acres of herbicide-tolerant wheat are already being grown across the Canadian prairies—more than 200,000 acres in 2005—without a sound of protest. Consumers, environmentalists, and farmers alike are conspicuous by their silence. Why the difference? Only that this wheat, called CDC Imagine, was created by chemical mutagenesis product itself, not because of the method that was used to generate that product. It is more important that we be able to trust our government agencies and other organizations to carefully scrutinize the safety and potential environmental impact of any new crop variety, regardless of whether it was generated by conventional breeding or genetic engineering, than it is to worry about the breeding method that was used to arrive at that product.

This does not mean, however, that there are not potential problems with GMOs. There are, in fact, two problems that are of particular concern to a growing number of farmers. Both problems

rather than by insertion of a bacterial gene. A product of the European-based chemical giant BASF, CDC Imagine was created by bathing wheat seeds with a chemical mutagen and selecting the surviving seedlings for tolerance to BASF's proprietary brand of imidazolinone herbicides.

So, we have two cases involving genetic modification at the level of a single gene. In Monsanto's case, the wheat was transformed with a gene for herbicide tolerance, while in the BASF case an existing wheat gene was mutated. Both methods end up with the same result, yet the Monsanto wheat faced stiff opposition based on the perception that a modified plant with herbicide tolerance posed a risk to human health and the environment. The Canadian Food Inspection Agency ruled that the gene modification in the BASF wheat posed "no significant risk" to either human health or the environment and it was approved. Either variety has the same potential for cross-pollinating with wild grasses or contaminating the wheat growing in a neighbor's field.

Some would say that our concern should be focused on the product, not the method. The question is whether the product—in this case, herbicide-tolerance in wheat—presents a measurable risk, rather than how that tolerance was bred into the plant. What do you think?

involve the potential for gene spread through cross-pollination. Many farmers still exercise the traditional practice of saving seed from each year's crop to use as seed for the following season. This is called **bin run seed** because the seed is taken from the farmer's own storage bin. Saving seed reduces costs for the farmer who does not have to purchase new seed each year and often results in the selection of seed that performs especially well within the conditions of a particular farm. If a genetically modified crop is planted in a neighboring field, there is the danger that pollen from the genetically modified crop will contaminate the non-modified plants.

Contamination can cause problems for the farmer who saves seed. The genes used to modify crop plants are patented, and farmers who wish to plant the modified crops must purchase new seed each year. They sign agreements with the seed company and are legally prohibited from saving seed. There are a number of ongoing court cases between seed companies and farmers, based on patented genes showing up in saved seed. The farmers claim the seed was contaminated through no doing of their own, while the seed companies claim the farmer is breaking patent law by saving seed that contains their patented gene. Most of these court cases have involved herbicide resistance in oilseed rape (or canola). Oilseed rape is a particularly precocious plant that readily cross-pollinates over long distances.

Organic farmers are also concerned about the spread of modified genes. Organic farmers must meet a number of conditions in order to have their crops certified as organic. One of those conditions prohibits the use of genetically modified crops (Figure 7.4). Organic farmers risk loss of their certification if their crops are contaminated with modified genes.

Both seed savers and organic growers are also concerned about the possibilities of a new technology called genetic use restriction technology (GURT), commonly referred to as "terminator technology" or "suicide seeds." This genetic technology causes plants to produce sterile seeds—the crop is normal in all respects

Figure 7.4 Due to the public's concern over the safety of GM foods, some manufacturers have chosen to label their foods as being free of genetically engineered ingredients.

except that the seeds produced by that crop will not germinate. Terminator technology could seriously erode the farmer's ability to save seed and increase their dependence on multinational corporations. This would be particularly serious in Third World countries, where an estimated 1.4 billion people depend on seed saving to feed themselves.

Terminator technology generated substantial protest when it was first brought to the public's attention in 1998. As a result, the technology was banned outright in several countries, and further research on the technology was banned under a moratorium issued by the United Nations convention of biological diversity in 2000. Although several large U.S. seed companies indicated they would not use the technology in their products, there is concern that research continues in the United States, which did not sign on to the moratorium.

Terminator technology may help to focus farmers, consumers, governments, and seed companies on the real risks and benefits of genetic modification. On the one hand, terminator technology would help seed companies protect their investment in modified crops, which can be substantial. On the other hand, it offers no agronomic benefit of any kind for farmers. It will likely be very difficult to balance the rights of seed companies against those of farmers and consumers, whose rights must also be protected.

A QUESTION OF RISK

Back in 1987, noted biochemist Daniel Koshland wrote in *Science* that "to be alive is to be at risk." We subject ourselves to risk in hundreds of ways every day of our lives, every time we step off the curb to cross a street, climb into an automobile or airplane, or eat food in a restaurant. Our recreation—Rollerblading, bicycling, skiing, swimming in shark-infested waters—and, in fact, virtually everything we do involves some level of risk. We accept that risk because each activity in some way makes our lives easier or better and we weigh the risks against the perceived benefit. But in each case, we also take steps to minimize risk. We install traffic lights at pedestrian crossings, we add more safety features to our automobiles and airplanes, we wear knee pads and helmets when we Rollerblade. Moreover, we attempt to educate our children and others about these risks and how to minimize our exposure.

In the end, we should approach biotechnology with the same caution. Both as individuals and as a society, we have to weigh the risks associated with biotechnology in all its forms, and especially GMOs, against the risks associated with conventional food production. And we have to take appropriate steps, including education, to minimize any risk. That means we should continue the necessary oversight to ensure that any new crop varieties, regardless of the method of production, meet acceptable guidelines for food safety and environmental protection.

Summary

Very early in the development of agriculture, farmers began what we now know as conventional plant breeding, simply by selecting the best seeds and crossing their best plants to improve the quality of grains and other food crops. In the twentieth century, however, a whole new arsenal of methods was developed by plant breeders, including double-crossed hybrids, mutations, embryo rescue, haploid breeding, and somaclonal variation. Each of these new methods has allowed the introduction of new traits into our food plants, and the products of these methods are considered acceptable by the public. Conventional breeding, however, always carries unknown genes into the new variety. By contrast, genetic modification (GM) is a far more precise technique, allowing the insertion of one specific gene expressing a single trait, yet this method is unacceptable to many.

A strong argument can be made that concern over food safety and protection of the environment should not be focused on the method. Herbicide tolerance, for example, can be introduced by both genetic modification and conventional breeding. If herbicide-resistance trait is a potential problem, should it matter how that trait was introduced into the crop? It would be more productive to focus on the safety of the product, rather than the method.

The question of food and environmental safety of any new crop really comes down to a question of risk management. We know that many foods contain potentially toxic substances and that genes naturally spread through the environment, but over the millennia we have learned to manage any potential risk and produce foods that are high-yielding, healthy, and nutritious. The real focus should be that all new crop varieties, regardless of how they are produced, continue to meet acceptable guidelines for food safety and environmental protection.

Accumulator species Plants that take up large amounts of heavy metal ions from the soil without injury.

Adventitious shoot (root) A shoot (or root) that arises where it is not normally expected, such as at the base of stem cuttings or from a clump of callus tissue in culture.

Alkaloid A nitrogen-containing chemical produced by plants that is physiologically active in vertebrates. Nicotine, caffeine, and morphine are examples of alkaloids.

Allele One of the two or more possible variants for a gene. A diploid organism contains two alleles, one contributed by each parent.

Anti-parallel The condition in double-stranded DNA in which the two strands with polarity run in opposite directions.

Apical meristem The growing point at the tip of a shoot or root.

Aseptic Free of contamination with microorganisms.

Backcross A cross between a hybrid and one of its parents (or a genetically equivalent organism).

Bacteriophage A virus that infects bacteria; also called simply "a phage."

Base A type of molecule, such as one of the five bases that make up nucleic acids: adenine, guanine, cytosine, thymine, and uracil.

Batch culture A bioreactor that is emptied and set up anew each time the reaction has run to completion.

Bin run seed Seed saved from a farmer's current crop to be used to plant the fields the following year, as opposed to buying new seed each season.

Bioengineering The application of engineering techniques to biological processes, such as large-scale cultures of fungi to produce drugs.

Biogas Methane gas that is generated by the microbial decomposition of organic matter in the absence of oxygen.

Bioreactor Any system that uses living organisms or enzymes to effect chemical changes, such as decomposition, decontamination, or production of chemical products.

Bioremediation The use of living organisms, usually bacteria, to decontaminate polluted soils.

Glossary

Biotechnology The use of living organisms to generate products for the use and benefit of humans.

Butanol A type of alcohol consisting of four carbon atoms per molecule.

Cellular respiration A sequence of metabolic reactions that converts sugars and other substrates to carbon dioxide and water in the presence of oxygen. The principal energy-generating metabolism in a cell.

Chemical mutagen A substance that induces mutations, or genetic changes, in the DNA of a living organism.

Codon A sequence of three adjacent nucleotides in DNA or RNA that comprises the genetic code for one amino acid in a protein.

Complementarity The property of base pairing in nucleic acid synthesis, in which the nucleotide sequence in the original strand is preserved in the newly formed complementary strand; a second round of copying restores the sequence of the original strand.

Continuous culture A bioreactor that is fed by a stream of nutrients and produces a continuous stream of effluent to be processed.

Conventional plant breeding Any method for producing new plant varieties that does not involve recombinant DNA.

Crown gall A cancerous growth on plants due to transformation of the host cells by the bacterium *Agrobacterium tumifaciens*.

Cyanogenic glycoside A chemical, found in some plants, that releases toxic hydrogen cyanide when the cells are disrupted.

DNA ligase An enzyme that catalyses the formation of strong covalent bonds along the sugar-phosphate backbone of DNA.

Edible vaccine A vaccine produced in a common food (such as bananas) that can be administered simply by eating the food.

Effervescence The property of producing large numbers of bubbles that rise to the surface with a fizzing sound, such as in beer or soda pop.

Electroporation The momentary induction of small pores in the membrane of a cell or protoplast by a brief pulse of electric current. It enables plant protoplasts to take up small pieces of DNA from the surrounding medium.

Embryo rescue A technique for culturing the hybrid embryo formed when two plants that do not normally mate are crossed.

Enterotoxin A toxin that has its effect in the gastrointestinal tract.

Fatty acid A long-chain hydrocarbon (composed of only carbon and hydrogen) with an oxygen-containing carboxylic acid group at one end. The principal component of fats and oils.

Feedstock The raw or starting material for an industrial manufacturing process. For example, crude oil is the feedstock for the production of gasoline and diesel fuel in a refinery.

Fermentation The metabolic breakdown of sugars and other substrates in the absence of oxygen. The product of fermentation is usually ethanol, lactic acid, or a similar chemical.

Fructose A six-carbon sugar molecule with a structure similar to glucose. Common table sugar (sucrose) is made up of one molecule each of glucose and fructose.

Gene The basic unit of heredity. A sequence of nucleotides in DNA that encodes the sequence of RNA, amino acids in a protein, or carries other instructions for the synthesis of proteins.

Gene gun A laboratory tool for shooting foreign DNA into plant cells. The technique is known as biolistics.

Genetically modified organism (GMO) Any organism whose genetic constitution has been successfully modified.

Genetic engineering The use of recombinant DNA technology to alter the genetic constitution of an organism.

Genetic modification (GM) Any change to the genetic constitution of an organism, although in common usage it refers specifically to changes involving recombinant DNA technology.

Genome The sum of all the genes in an organism.

Glufosinate An herbicide that kills plants by blocking the incorporation of inorganic nitrogen into organic molecules.

Glycolysis A sequence of enzymatic reactions in a cell that convert one molecule of glucose to two molecules of pyruvic acid. It is common to both cellular respiration and fermentation. The difference between respiration and fermentation is in the fate of the pyruvic acid.

Glossary

Glyphosate A herbicide that kills plants by blocking the synthesis of the aromatic amino acids, which are characterized by having a chemical ring as part of their structure.

Helicase An enzyme that separates the two strands of double-stranded DNA during replication.

Hybrid The offspring or progeny from two organisms differing by one or more genes.

Hydrocarbon A molecule made up of only the elements carbon and hydrogen. Methane (CH_4) is the simplest hydrocarbon. Diesel fuel and gasoline are mixtures of several hydrocarbons.

Hydrogen bond Weak forces that hold molecules together by sharing a hydrogen ion. The hydrogen is normally shared between two oxygen and/or nitrogen atoms.

Inbred line A genetically pure line that breeds true. Inbred lines usually arise through self-pollination and selection.

Ionizing radiation Radiation that has sufficient energy to cause permanent changes in molecules.

Landrace A variety of any agricultural crop that has become adapted to the microclimate of a particular limited area through generations of selection.

Marker gene A gene for a trait such as antibiotic resistance that enables technicians to identify cells that have been successfully transformed.

Metabolite Any chemical that participates in the chemical reactions that occur within a cell or organism.

Micropropagation The technique for reproducing plants asexually through tissue culture.

Microshoot The small shoots that are produced by micropropagation.

Molecular farming (pharming) The use of genetically modified plants as bioreactors to produce molecules that plants do not normally produce. When the molecule has pharmaceutical value, the process is called molecular pharming.

Mutation breeding The introduction, via conventional breeding, of genes modified by inducing mutations with ionizing radiation or chemical mutagens.

Nanotechnologist Researchers who work at the nanometer scale (1 nanometer = 1 billionth of a meter).

Nucleotide A molecule composed of a nitrogen base, a sugar, and a phosphate group. The basic building block of nucleic acids.

Open pollinated Pollinated by natural means.

Osmosis The diffusion of water across a membrane.

Overexpression A term that describes what happens when a gene is engineered to produce more than normal amounts of the protein that it codes for.

Phytochelatins A small protein that prevents heavy metal toxicity by sequestering the metal ions and storing them in the large central vacuole of the cell.

Phytoprospecting The use of accumulator species of plants as an indication of the presence of particular metals in the environment.

Phytoremediation The use of plants to decontaminate polluted soils, especially soils contaminated with heavy metals.

Plasmid A small piece of circular DNA found in bacteria and in the mitochondria and chloroplasts of animal and plant cells.

Polyhydroxyalkoanate (PHA) A biodegradable plastic synthesized by certain bacteria.

Protoplast A plant cell that has been stripped of its cell wall, leaving the cell membrane intact. A naked plant cell.

Pyruvic acid A three-carbon molecule that serves as a precursor for fermentation and respiration products such as ethanol and carbon dioxide.

Recombinant DNA A fragment of DNA containing the DNA from two different species spliced together in the laboratory. A plant cell naturally infected with *Agrobacterium* also contains recombinant DNA.

Restriction enzyme A substance that cuts double-stranded DNA at the site of a particular base sequence.

Reverse engineering The synthesis, in the laboratory, of an artificial gene or a strand of DNA matching the amino acid sequence of a known protein.

Reverse transcriptase An enzyme that transcribes RNA into DNA.

Glossary

Selection A technique for plant improvement in which the best seed from each crop representing a particular trait is saved for planting the next generation or making the next cross.

Sequester To withdraw or tie up.

Shoot tip culture A technique for culturing the growing region at the tip of a plant stem in order to induce the formation of multiple microshoots.

Somaclonal variation Mutations that arise during micropropagation.

Somatic hybrid A hybrid formed asexually by the fusion of two or more protoplasts.

Totipotent The capacity for any plant cell or tissue to develop into a fully competent mature plant.

Transcription The assembly of an RNA molecule complementary to a strand of DNA.

Transformation The transfer of genes from one organism to another.

Transgenic An organism that has been genetically transformed.

Translation The assembly of a protein on a ribosome in accordance with the sequence of nucleotides in a strand of messenger RNA.

Triglyceride A fat or oil molecule consisting of three fatty acids attached to a molecule of glycerol.

Vector In genetics, a means for carrying DNA into a cell. The *Agrobacterium* plasmid is an example of a vector that is used to transform plant cells.

Vegetative reproduction Plant reproduction that does not involve the union of sperm and eggs.

Bibliography

Alberts, B., A. Johnson, J. Lewis, et al. *Molecular Biology of the Cell.* New York: Garland Science, 2002.

Bud, R. *The Uses of Life: A History of Biotechnology.* Cambridge, England: Cambridge University Press, 1993.

Cummins, R., and B. Lilliston. *Genetically Engineered Food: A Self-Defense Guide for Consumers.* New York: Marlowe & Co., 2000.

Grace, Eric R. *Biotechnology Unzipped.* Toronto: Trifolium Books, 1997.

Hart, K. *Eating in the Dark.* New York: Vintage Books, 2002.

Hopkins, W. G., and N. P. A. Hüner. *Introduction to Plant Physiology,* 3rd ed. New York: John Wiley & Sons, 2004.

McHughen, A. *Pandora's Picnic Basket: The Potential and Hazards of Genetically Modified Foods.* Oxford: Oxford University Press, 2000.

Kreuzer, H., and A. Massey. *Recombinant DNA and Biotechnology.* Washington, DC: ASM Press, 2001.

Plasterk, R. H. A. "RNA Silencing: The Genome's Immune System." *Science* 296 (2002): 1263–1265.

Pringle, P. *Food, Inc.: Mendel to Monsanto—The Promises and Perils of the Biotech Harvest.* New York: Simon & Schuster, 2003.

Raven, P. H., R. F. Evert, S. E. Eichhorn. *Biology of Plants.* New York: Worth Publishers, 1999.

Tagliaferro, L. *Genetic Engineering: Progress or Peril?* New York: Lerner Publications, 1997.

Thieman, W. J., and M. A. Palladino. *Introduction to Biotechnology.* San Francisco: Benjamin Cummings, 2004.

Turner, N. J., and A. F. Szczawinski. *Common Poisonous Plants and Mushrooms of North America.* Portland, OR: Timber Press, 1991.

Watson, J. D. *The Double Helix.* New York: Atheneum, 1968.

Further Reading

Hart, K. *Eating in the Dark*. New York: Vintage Books, 2002.

Pringle, P. *Food, Inc.: Mendel to Monsanto—The Promises and Perils of the Biotech Harvest*. New York: Simon & Schuster, 2003.

Tagliaferro, L. *Genetic Engineering: Progress or Peril?* New York: Lerner Publications, 1997.

Watson, J. D. *The Double Helix*. New York: Atheneum, 1968.

Web Sites

Canadian Renewable Fuels Association

http://www.greenfuels.org

This site has many links to both Canadian and American renewable fuels sites.

Cold Spring Harbor DNA Learning Center

http://www.dnalc.org

A student-friendly resource with links to current topics in gene cloning and recombinant DNA techniques.

Gene Gun

http://www.nysaes.cornell.edu/pubs/press/1999/genegun.html

This site describes the origins of the helium-powered gene gun.

International Survey of Herbicide-Resistant Weeds

http://www.weedscience.org/in.asp

With extensive use of herbicides and herbicide-resistant crops, the development of herbicide-resistant weeds is an increasing problem. This interesting Website tracks the origin and distribution of herbicide-resistant weeds.

Molecular Farming

http://www.molecularfarming.com

Well-constructed site with extensive links to other sites both for and against genetic engineering.

National Center for Biotechnology Information

http://www.ncbi.nlm.nih.gov

Website sponsored by the National Library of Medicine and the National Institutes of Health that is useful for a general perspective on biotechnology (with an emphasis on human and animal applications).

Nobel Prize in Physiology or Medicine

http://www.nobel.se/medicine

Information on past recipients of the Nobel Prize.

"RNAi." *Nova* **(Public Broadcasting System)**

http://www.pbs.org/wgbh/nova/sciencenow/3210/02.html

Provides animated video and links to questions and answers.

Terminator Technology and Transgenic Crops

http://filebox.vt.edu/cals/cses/chagedor/terminator.html

A brief description of how the genetic restriction technology works. Includes a link to the Transgenic Crops Homepage (http://filebox.vt.edu/cals/cses/chagedor/crops.html), which provides access to other useful information about transgenic crops.

Index

Accumulator species, 32–35
Acetic acid, fermentation and, 19
Acetyl-CoA, PHAs and, 100–102
Actinomucor elegans, 20
Adaptive advantages, 119–121
Advantages of GMO crops, 111
Adventitious shoots, 36
Aflatoxins, peanuts and, 117
Agrobacterium tumefaciens, 77–79, 108
Alaska, bioremediation in, 28
Alcohols, 5, 7
Alkali poisoning, 32
Alkaloids, in foods, 116–117
Amino acids, 56, 80–82
Ammonium perchlorate, 27
Amylase, 5, 22
Antibiotics, 10, 21, 23, 62, 64
Antibodies, 98–99
Antifreeze genes, 115
Antiparallel, defined, 54
Apical meristems, 38
Arabidopsis thaliana, 101
Arntzen, C.J., 98–99
Aseptic technique, 17, 36
Aspergillus niger, 22
Aspergillus oryzae, 20
Astralgus, 32
Auxins, crown gall and, 77–79
Axillary buds, 38–39

Bacillus thuringiensis (Bt) protein,
    89–92, 116
Backcrossing, 111
Bacteria, 61–62, 114
Bacteriophages, 60–62
Base pairing, 52–55
Batch culture, defined, 21
Beer, 4–5
Berg, Paul, 61–62
Beta-carotene, 22, 96
Bialaphos, 80–82
Bin run seed, 122
Biodegradable plastics, 100–102

Biodiesel, 41–43, 44–46
Bioengineering, defined, 8
Biofuels, 23, 40–44, 47
Biogas, 41, 44
Biolistics, 76, 77
Bioreactors, 25, 26, 27, 41, 97–102
Bioremediation, 26–28, 29
Biotechnology, defined, 8, 10
Blind staggers disease, 32
Boyer, Herbert, 62
Brassica species, 93
Brazil, 24, 43–44
Breadmaking, 4–5, 7
Butanol, fermentation and, 16
Butterflies, Bt and, 90–91
Butyl rubber, 16

Caffeine, toxicity of, 117
Canadian Food Inspection Agency
    (CFIA), 118, 121
Cane sugar, 24, 43–44
Canola, 93, 94, 122
Catalysts, enzymes as, 24
Cattails, bioremediation and, 26
Cattle, 32, 34, 40
CDC Imagine wheat, 120–121
cDNA, 70–71
Cellular respiration, 17–19
Cellulose, gasohol and, 43–44
Certification of organic crops, 122
Chargaff, Erwin, 50–52
Cheese, 5–7
Chelation, 33
Chemical mutagens, 73,
    120–121
Chemicals, 20–22, 97–102
Chitinase, viral resistance and, 92
Citric acid, 21, 22
Citric acid cycle, 18, 19
Clones, defined, 35
Codons, protein synthesis and, 57
Cohen, Stanley, 62
Colorado potato beetles, 89, 90, 91

Competitive advantages, 119–121
Complementarity, 53–55, 59, 67
Complementary DNA (cDNA), 70–71
Contamination, seeds and, 122
Continuous culture, defined, 21
Conventional plant breeding
   acceptance of, 106
   disadvantages of, 109–111
   herbicide tolerance and, 120–121
   history of, 107–108
   pesticide tolerance and, 119
   process overview, 108–109
   trait development by, 111–114
Cooking oils, 44, 46, 100
Corn, 76, 96, 108, 110
Corn steep liquor, 23
Cotton, 101–102
Crick, Francis, 52–53
Crossing, 108–110
Cross-pollination, 122
Crown gall, 76–79
CryIAb, 91
Cyanogenic glycosides, 116
Cytokinins, crown gall and, 77–79

Denitrifying bacteria, 26
Deoxyribonucleic acid (DNA). *See* DNA
Department of Agriculture, U.S., 118, 119
Disease resistance, 89–92
DNA
   genes and, 54–56
   insertion into plant cells, 75–79
   modern biotechnology and, 60–66
   overview of, 50–54
   presence of in all foods, 114, 116
   proteins and, 56–60
DNA fingerprinting, 65–66, 74
DNA ligase, 54, 74
DNA polymerase, 55, 74
Domestication, 4–5
Double helix model, 52–54

EcoRI enzyme, 61–62, 63
Edible vaccines, 99–100
Effervescence, citric acid and, 22
Electrophoresis, 66
Electroporation, 75–76, 77
Embryo rescue, 112–113
Enolpyruvyl-shikimate-3-phosphate synthase (EPSPS), 80, 82
Enterotoxins, 89–92
Environmental Protection Agency (EPA), 10
Environmental safety, 119–124
Enzymes, 22, 24–25. *See also specific enzymes*
Ereky, Karl, 14
Erucic acid, 93
Escherichia coli (E. coli), 28, 61–62, 99
Ethanol, 19, 21, 23–24, 43–44
Ethyl methane sulfonate (EMS), 73
Explants, micropropagation and, 38
Exxon *Valdez*, 28

Farming, molecular, 97–102, 120
Fatty acids, 41, 42, 46, 93–95
Feedstocks, 8
Fermentation
   biodegradable plastics and, 102
   butanol production and, 16
   feedstock production and, 8
   gasohol and, 44
   glycerol production and, 14–15
   industrial production and, 20–25
   Louis Pasteur and, 14
   overview of, 5, 17–19
Fingerprinting, DNA, 65–66, 74
Fish genes, tomatoes and, 115
Flavr-Savr tomatoes, 115
Fleming, Alexander, 23
Flounder genes, 115
Flower coloration, 87–88
Food and Drug Administration (FDA), 118
Food safety, 114–117, 118

Index

Forensics, 65–66
Franklin, Rosalind, 53
Fungi, 7–8, 9. *See also specific species*
Fungicides, 80–81
Fusarium infections, 9
Fusion of protoplasts, 75

Gall, 76–79
Gasohol, 43–44
Gels, 66
Gene guns, 76, 77
Genes, overview of, 54–56
Gene spread, 119–122
Genetically modified organisms
    (GMOs), defined, 8
Genetic engineering, 8
Genetic modification (GM), 8
Genetic reassortment, 35
Genetic use restriction technology
    (GURT), 122–124
Genetic variability, 109
Genomes, defined, 56
Gibberellin, 22, 112
Glucose, fermentation and, 5
Glucose isomerase, 24
Glucosinolates, 93, 117
Glufosinate, 80–82
Glycerin, biofuels and, 46
Glycerol, 14–15, 19, 21, 41, 42
Glycine max, 20, 44–46, 81
Glycolysis, 17–18
Glyphosate, 79–82, 86–87, 120–121
GM crops, criticisms of
    bacterial consumption, 114
    DNA consumption, 114, 116
    gene spread, 119–122
    myths, 115
    patenting, 109
    pesticide consumption, 116
    precautionary principle, 118–119
    risk assessment, 124–125
    terminator technology, 122–124
    toxin presence as, 116–118

Goitrogens, 117
Golden rice, 94–96
Greenpeace, 107
Griseofulvin, 21
Groundwater, 27
Gun cotton, 16

Haploid breeding, 113
Heavy metals, 26, 32
Helicase, 54, 55
Helices, 52–54
Hemophilus influenzae, 61
Hepatitis B antigen, 98–99
Herbicide tolerance
    criticisms of GMOs and, 119
    genetic engineering and, 79–82
    protein structure and, 56–57
    public resistance to, 120–121
    tobacco, 10
    value of, 86–87
Heritage varieties, 109
High-fructose syrups, 24–25
Hind III enzyme, 61
Human immunodeficiency virus
    (HIV), 71
Human toxicity, 82
Hybridization, 75, 108–109
Hydrocarbons, 28
Hydrogenation, 93–95
Hydrogen bonds, 52–55

Immunizations, 98–100
Inbred lines, 108–109
Indicator species, 32–33
Insecticides, 88–89, 89–92
Insulin, 63
Invertase, 22
Ionizing radiation, 73

Jorgensen, Rich, 87–88

Krebs cycle, 18, 19
Labeling, GMOs and, 123

Lactic acid, 14, 19, 20
Lactobacillus, 20
Lake Ontario, 28
Landfills, methane and, 40–41
Landraces, 109
Lepidopterans, Bt and, 90–91, 116
Liberty, 80–82
Libraries, cDNA, 70–71
Ligase, 54, 74
Lipids, 95
Locoweed, 32
Lodging, 112, 113
Lysine, feedstock and, 96

Maize, transformation of, 76
Mannitol, protoplasts and, 73–75
Marker genes, 64, 65
Marquis wheat, 108
Marsh gas, 40–41
Measles, edible vaccines and, 100
Messenger RNA (mRNA), 57, 58, 59,
    70–71, 87–88
Metabolites, production of, 20–25
Metals, 26, 32
Methane, biofuels and, 40–41
Methylation, 60
Microbiology, Pasteur and, 14
Micropropagation, 36–40, 113–114
Molecular farming, 97–102, 120
Monarch butterflies, Bt and, 90–91
mRNA, 57, 58, 59, 70–71, 87–88
Mutagens, chemical, 73
Mutation breeding, 112
Mutations, 71–73, 112

Nanotechnology, 76
National Center for Biotechnology
    Information, 10
Natural gas, methane and, 40
Nature, 52–54, 90
Neuberg, C.A., 14–15
Nickel, phytomining and, 34
Nitroglycerin, 16

Nobel, Alfred, 16–17
Nobel Prize, 17, 61, 62
Norwalk virus, 99
Nucleotides, 50, 51, 59
Nutrition, improving, 93–96

Oil refineries, 26–27
Oils, 41–44, 46, 93–95, 100
Oilseed rape, 93, 94, 122
Open-pollination, 109
Orchids, 39
Organic farming, 116, 122
Origins of biotechnology, 4–7, 14
Osmosis, protoplasts and, 73–75
Overexpression, defined, 80
Oxygen, 18–19, 44

Pandora's Picnic Basket, 114
Papain, 24
Paper mills, 34
Pasteur, Louis, 14, 15
Pasteurization, 114
Pathogens, 39–40
Pauling, Linus, 52–54
PCR. *See* Polymerase chain reaction
Peanuts, aflatoxins and, 117
Pectinase, 22
Penicillin, 21, 23
Penicillium chrysogenum, 23
Perchlorate, 27
Pesticides, 116, 119
Petroleum products, 28
Petunias, pigmentation and, 87–88
Phages, 60–62
Pharming, molecular, 97–102, 120
Phytoaccumulation, 34–35
Phytochelatins, 33
Phytoprospecting, 32–33
Phytoremediation, 32–35
Plant cell transformation, 73, 75–76
Plant oils, biofuels and, 41–44
Plasmids, 62–64, 65, 79
Plastics, biodegradable, 100–102

Index

Pollination, 88–90, 109, 122
Polyhydroxyalkanoates (PHAs),
 100–102
Polymerase chain reaction (PCR),
 65–66, 74
Polymerases, 55, 74
Potatoes
 alkaloids in, 116–117, 118
 disease resistance and, 75
 gasohol and, 44
 micropropagation and, 40
 molecular farming and, 99
 somaclonal variation (SCV) and,
  114
Precautionary principle, 118–119
Precision, as advantage, 111
Prince William Sound, 28
Probes, fingerprinting and, 66
Productivity, defined, 9, 92, 92–94
Proteases, 22, 117
Proteins, 56–60, 89–92
Protoplasts, 73–75
Pseudomonas, 28
Pyruvic acid, 18–19

Radiation, ionizing, 73
Rapeseed, 93
Reassortment, 35
Recombinant DNA (rDNA), 8, 61–62,
 67
Rennet, industrial production of, 22
Rennin, 6, 7, 8, 24
Replica plating, 64
Replication, 54, 62–64, 74
Resistance, 88–92. *See also* Herbicide
 tolerance
Respiration, 17–19
Restriction enzymes, 60–62, 62–64,
 65–66, 67
Retroviruses, 70–71
Reverse engineering, 71
Reverse transcriptase, 70–71
Rhizopus, 20

Riboflavin, 22
Ribonucleic acid (RNA), 50, 57
Ribosomes, 59
Rice, Golden, 94–96
Risk, assessment of, 124–125
RNA interference (RNAi), 87–88
RNA silencing, 87–88
Roundup, 79–82, 86–87, 120–121
Rubber, synthetic, 16
Russet Burbank potatoes, 114

Saccharomyces cerevisiae, 5, 19
Safety, 114–117, 118, 119–124
Salix species, 35
Saturation, 93–95
Sedges, bioremediation and, 26
Seed oils, 41, 93–94
Selection, 64, 108
Selenium, 32, 34
Sequestration, 33
Serotonin, bananas and, 117
Sewage treatment plants, 40
Shoot-tip culture, 38
Shotgun biolistics, 76, 77
Silencing, 87–88
Silos, methane and, 41
Smith, Hamilton, 61–62
Solanine, 116–117, 118
Solanum tuberosum, 75
Somaclonal variations, 40, 113–114
Somatic hybridization, 75
Soybeans, 20, 44–46, 81
Soy sauce, 20
Starches, gasohol and, 43–44
Start codons, 59
Stearic acid, 94
Sterile technique, 17, 36
Sterility, 122–124
Sticky ends, 62
Streptomyces hygroscopicus, 80–82
Sufu, 20
Sugar cane, 24, 43–44
Sugar-phosphate backbone, 52–55

Suicide seeds, 122–124
Sunflower oil, biofuels and, 41
Suppression, RNA and, 87–88
Swamp gas, 40–41
Sweet potatoes, 44

Tempeh, 20
Temperature, PCR and, 74
Teosinte, 108
Terminator technology, 122–124
Thallium, phytomining and, 34
Thermal properties, 101–102
Thlaspi species, 33
Ti plasmids, 79
Tissue culture, 36
Tobacco, 10, 97–98
Tobacco mosaic virus (TMV), 72
Tomatoes, 115
Totipotency, 38
Toxicity, human, 82
Toxins, in all foods, 116–118
Trace elements, 34
Transcription, 57
Transfer RNA (tRNA), 58, 59
Transformation
    of bacteria, 62–63, 64
    of plant cells, 73, 75–76, 76–79
Translation, 58
Triazine resistance, 56–57
Triglycerides, 41, 42, 95

Uniformity, clones and, 35–36

Vaccines, 98–100
Variability, genetic, 109
Variations, somaclonal, 40
Vegetative reproduction, 36
Vetch, 32
Vinegar, 19
Viruses, 39–40, 60–62, 70–72, 92
Visualization, 66
Vitamins, 22, 96

Waste management, 26
Watson, James, 52–53
Weeds, control of, 86–87
Weizmann, Chaim, 16
Weizmann process, 16, 17
Wetlands, 26
Wheat, 108, 112, 120–121
White, Phillip, 36
Wilkins, Maurice, 53
Willows, 35
Wines, 5

Yeasts, fermentation and, 5
Yields, 9, 92–94

Zea mays, 76
Zymology, defined, 14
Zymotechnology, 14

Picture Credits

William G. Hopkins received a B.A. in biology from Wesleyan University and a Ph.D. in botany from Indiana University. His post-doctoral training was conducted at Brookhaven National Laboratories. He has taught at Bryn Mawr College and the University of Western Ontario, where he is now professor emeritus (Biology). Dr. Hopkins has taught primarily in the areas of plant physiology and cell biology, was responsible for design and implementation of an honors program in cell biology, and served many years as an undergraduate counselor. In 1988, Dr. Hopkins was awarded the university's Gold Medal for Excellence in Teaching. His research and publications have focused on the role of light and temperature in plant development, the organization of chlorophyll-protein complexes, and energy transformations in chloroplasts. Dr. Hopkins has been a contributing author to two high school biology textbooks and is the senior author of *Introduction to Plant Physiology*, a textbook published by John Wiley & Sons and now in its third edition.